HOW TO
SHARE YOUR FAITH
WITH OTHERS

HOW TO
SHARE YOUR FAITH
WITH OTHERS

A Good News Guidebook

Father Joseph T. Sullivan

Diocesan Director
Office of Evangelization
Burlington, Vermont

Liguori

LIGUORI, MISSOURI

Published by Liguori Publications
Liguori, Missouri
http://www.liguori.org

Library of Congress Cataloging-in-Publication Data

Sullivan, Joseph T.
    How to share your faith with others : a good news guidebook / Joseph T. Sullivan.—1st ed.
          p. cm.
    ISBN 0-7648-0665-3 (pbk.)
    1. Evangelistic work—Miscellanea. 2. Witness bearing (Christianity)—Miscellanea. 3. Catholic Church—Doctrines—Miscellanea. I. Title.

BX2347.4 .S85 2000
248'.5—dc21   00-042830

Contents

Introduction

Evangelization is the essential mission of the Church. Jesus Christ commissioned his apostles and followers to "teach all nations." They are to communicate the "Good News," the Gospel, to every person on the face of the earth. The challenge is the same today as it was after Christ's Resurrection when he sent his disciples to bring this great news of God's unfathomable love.

Evangelizers are needed in every age to carry the torch of faith from one generation to the next. Jesus Christ is the Light of the World. Jesus also taught that his followers were to enlighten their friends, family members, relatives, neighbors—everyone.

A high-school teenager was asked if she knew what evangelization was all about. She replied, "No," and shook her head. The same is true for countless numbers of people.

"Evangelization means sharing our faith in Jesus Christ with others."

The teenager said, "Oh!"

It is our prayer that this book will assist all the baptized in their essential mission, sharing their love and faith in Jesus Christ with the millions who are not yet Christians in name and in fact, and bringing to them the Good News of Jesus Christ who said: "I am the way, and the truth, and the life. No one comes to the Father except through me" (Jn 14:6). We all must be explicit and untiring promoters of Christ's unique and universal role as the world's savior.

The body of this book contains twenty-five short chapters in question-and-answer format. "Evangelization made easy" is the reason behind these "short-take" chapters and pointed answers to some complex questions. Together these chapters give an overview of the process of evangelization. This book can be used as a book of self-preparation, as part of a series of training sessions, or just as a personal introduction to the work of making disciples for Christ. Each chapter covers important topics such as the what and why of evangelization, how to overcome reticence in spreading the Good News, and also covers important aspects of the Catholic faith that may arise in discussions with those seeking either to return to the Church or those who want to find out about it for the first time.

At the end of each chapter are additional topics called "Something Extra" that give more detailed and condensed information, for example, "What are the goals of Catholic evangelization?" "What do Catholics believe about the Eucharist?" or "How can a parish roll out the welcome mat for new or returning Catholics?" These added sections can be skipped or can be read at another time.

At the end of the book are several examples of copy that can be used as part of handout cards or leaflets as part of an evangelization effort. (Plus—some of the lists or parts of the "Something Extra" information can also be made into leaflets or informational brochures, with some minor changes, of course.) Finally, there is an extensive list of resources that can further support any evangelization endeavor. All told, these materials are designed to introduce the essence of the topic of evangelization in a simple and easy format so that all can become sharers of the Good News.

HOW TO
SHARE YOUR FAITH
WITH OTHERS

CHAPTER ONE

Proclaim

How do you evangelize?

You proclaim Jesus Christ!

Show me. Let's have an example.

A young lady leaves her office and walks down the corridor. The man ahead of her drops a package, and exclaims in frustration, "Jesus Christ." He thoughtlessly uses the name of Jesus as an expletive. She says, "May his holy name be praised." The man asks, "What? What did you say?" She replies, "You said, Jesus Christ, and I answered, may his holy name be praised." Quietly, she looks him in the eye, and he realizes his choice of words is inappropriate, that he has offended her religious sensitivity.

That's evangelization?

Part of it. Christ is proclaimed.

How about another example?

A man fashions a small alpine shrine with a crucifix. He hangs it on a tree in front of his house.

That's evangelization? It seems like advertising, even the flaunting of his faith.

Advertising has for its purpose to gain attention and to influence—usually to sell products or services. Evangelization has no commercial purpose. It seeks to reflect on the outside what is entertained on the inside. The man's faith in Christ is demonstrated. Christ is proclaimed.

Is this not flaunting his faith, wearing it on his sleeve?

No. In his way, this man proclaims Jesus Christ. He is actually countering our secular society, where God is left out of so many aspects of life. Visit one of the poorest countries in this hemisphere, Haiti, and observe pickup trucks painted colorfully and named after Jesus and the saints. Travel to Austria and Switzerland, and see images of Jesus and the saints on the outside walls of homes. The culture, the common way of life, in some other countries, includes the proclamation of Christ naturally, gracefully, and realistically.

So you think this helps the cause of evangelization?

Out of sight, out of mind. Where there are so many attractions and distractions in our world, it just may be that people are not focusing on the issues of human origin and destiny. They are like Martha in the gospel incident. Jesus visited her home in Bethany. She was fussing about with many details, but Mary, her sister, sat at Christ's feet and gave him her full attention. You may recall that Jesus said that Mary had made the better choice. Proclaiming Jesus Christ and focusing the world's full attention on him is an indispensable part of meeting the challenge of evangelization.

You're not going to convert anyone merely by erecting outdoor shrines and correcting expletives, are you?

True! However, there has to be a first step in a thousand-mile journey.

From the looks of things, this is more like a million-mile journey. A young lady walking down an office corridor and a man displaying an alpine shrine will have to be multiplied many times over before you capture the attention of a great number of people.

There is no need to be intimidated. The Church grew from small and humble beginnings. Just as the shepherd boy David was able to slay the giant Goliath with only a sling and a stone because God was on his side, so Christians must have confidence in the same measure. Jesus started with twelve apostles and some seventy or more disciples. When he ascended to heaven Jesus assured them: "You will receive power when the Holy Spirit has come upon you; and you will be my witnesses in Jerusalem, in all Judea and Samaria, and to the ends of the earth" (Acts 1:8).

There has to be more in the evangelization process than merely proclaiming Jesus Christ. You can print his name on billboards from coast to coast but it is probably not going to mean much to most people.

Proclaiming Jesus Christ includes personal endorsement. Men and women are encouraged to buy products or engage services when celebrities endorse them. Movies stars, sports heroes, and public figures lend their names in advertising all the time. People say to themselves that there must be something to this endorsement. Christians just do not put forth their names. They demonstrate their faith in Christ. This is powerful and persuasive.

So good example leads men and women to become Christians? Maybe some are impressed, but not everyone.

Good example is a powerful and effective agent for change. In the early centuries after Christ, people remarked, "See how the Christians love one another." Folks recognize goodness when they see it, and especially, when they experience it. They are impressed by the sincerity and goodness of those around them. How well Christ and his teachings are embodied in the lives of neighbors, fellow workers, friends, and family is an indicator of successful evangelization. There are more than a billion Christians worldwide, including Catholics, Orthodox, and Protestants, who can potentially live this example.

Yes, but we are entering the third millennium of Christianity, and four-fifths of the world population is not Christian.

That is true, but Jesus, the first evangelizer, told this story about sowing seeds. Some fell on rocky soil, some were choked by weeds, and some were eaten by birds. Still others fell on good soil and grew and were fruitful. Christ explained that the seeds were, in effect, the word of God. He was a realist. Not everyone is receptive to God's word. Seeds have difficulty growing in harsh and hostile environments. Mindful of the challenges, Christ commissioned his followers to evangelize.

Sooner or later there has to be a more in-depth presentation of Christianity. Proclaiming Christ has to entail explanations and answers to questions. You may be able to pique curiosity with billboards and other proclamations. Folks want to know the underlying rationale.

That's right. "Always be ready to make your defense to anyone who demands from you an accounting for the hope that is in you" (1 Pet 3:15).

When does the evangelizer go from witnessing to explaining?

A Church document relating to evangelization says this: "The Good News proclaimed by the witness of a good life sooner or later has to be proclaimed by the Word of Life. There is no true evangelization if the name, the teaching, the life, the promises, the kingdom and the mystery of Jesus of Nazareth, the Son of God are not proclaimed" (*A Summary: On Evangelization in the Modern World*, §22). Unless there is direct focus on Jesus, there is no true evangelization. People have to hear the word. They have to come to know Jesus and his role in God's plan.

So Jesus is like other famous religious leaders recorded in history?

No. He is the central figure in all history. He is a divine Person, God and man.

Something Extra

What do Catholics really believe? Can you tell me in a nutshell?

The core of the Catholic faith can be found in several creeds which are short statements of beliefs. The Nicene Creed is the formula that Catholics recite at Sunday Mass:

> We believe in one God,
>> the Father, the Almighty,
>> maker of heaven and earth,
>> of all that is seen and unseen.
> We believe in one Lord, Jesus Christ,
>> the only Son of God,
>> eternally begotten of the Father.
>> God from God, Light from Light,
>> true God from true God,
>> begotten, not made,
>> one in Being with the Father.
>> Through him all things were made.
> For us men and for our salvation
>>> he came down from heaven:
>> by the power of the Holy Spirit
>>> he was born of the the Virgin Mary,
>>> and became man.
> For our sake he was crucified under Pontius Pilate;
>> he suffered, died, and was buried.
>> On the third day he rose again
>>> in fulfillment of the Scriptures;
>> he ascended into heaven
>>> and is seated at the right hand of the Father.

He will come again in glory to judge
    the living and the dead,
     and his kingdom will have no end.
We believe in the Holy Spirit, the Lord,
    the giver of life,
     who proceeds from the Father
     and the Son.
With the Father and the Son
    he is worshiped and glorified.
He has spoken through the Prophets.
We believe in one holy catholic and
    apostolic Church.
We acknowledge one baptism for the
    forgiveness of sins.
We look for the resurrection of the dead,
    and the life of the world to come. Amen.

CHAPTER TWO

Jesus Christ: A Five-Minute Presentation

Let's pretend that I am really interested in Jesus Christ and his teachings. You have awakened my curiosity. You have five minutes to tell me about him.

So this is my golden opportunity. I have five minutes to sum up world history from the beginning of time, the shortest amount of time to tell you about God's intervention in our world.

Maybe it's my lunch hour. I have to get back to the office.

First of all, a prayer is in order.

Lord, send your grace to this person. Enlighten the mind and dispose the will. May the Holy Spirit touch the soul and flood it with light. Lead the soul to repentance and bless it with the gift of faith. Amen.

Don't delay. The prayer is eating into your allotted time.

John, the Baptist, preached repentance and belief. Jesus echoed John's theme. Repent, and believe! A person has to want to believe and to accept the consequences of knowing God's holy will.

The clock is ticking. Go on.

In the beginning God created everything—the sun, the moon, the stars, the planets and, of course, our Earth. From nothing, God brought the animate and the inanimate into existence—minerals, gasses, and solids—plants, animals, and humans. The first people, Adam and Eve, were blessed with a garden of paradise where all things lived in harmony. Their gifts included freedom from sickness and disease, from want and suffering. They were to obey God, particularly not to eat from the Tree of Knowledge. They gave in to temptation, ate from the forbidden fruit, defied God. This was catastrophic. Eating the fruit was almost incidental. Their defiance and disobedience was monumental. They lost their preternatural gifts, and their consciences became heavy with guilt. Driven from paradise, plunged into despair, Adam and Eve were promised a Redeemer by a merciful God. This Messiah was to lift their overburdened spirits and open the gates to eternal happiness.

This sounds familiar. It is the Genesis story, isn't it?

Yes, it is. The Bible is a written account of God's communication, of God's relationship with mankind. The books in the Old Testament tell of God's ongoing dialogue. Some stories are well known: the Tower of Babel, Noah and his Ark, the Ten Commandments, and so on. Adam's and Eve's original sin lost their special gifts for posterity. The human will was weakened and the mind was darkened. The books in the

Bible relate how people strayed and God brought them back.

So what else is new? Isn't this happening all the time? History continually repeats itself, doesn't it?

Yes. God decided to express his love in a direct way when he chose Abraham to be the father of his "Chosen People," the Jews. Read the stories of God's dialogue with Abraham, Isaac, Jacob, Joseph, Moses, Saul, Solomon, David. The Jews were in exile, subject to hostilities from surrounding tribes, carried off to Babylon, and made slaves in Egypt.

I saw the old movie, Cecil B. DeMille's "The Ten Commandments." Moses led his people out of Egypt and across the Red Sea. They wandered in the desert for forty years.

During these long years, God solidified his relationship with them. He articulated his holy will with the Ten Commandments. There was a special covenant. They were his people. He was their God. Gradually, through the years, and through the prophets, God's promise to send a Redeemer, a Messiah, was made clear. Their religion, their relationship with God, was in great expectation for the long-awaited Messiah.

Many people know these stories in bits and pieces. History is not coordinated in their minds. They do not see a thread weaving through the centuries.

At a point of time (let's have a drum roll) some 2000 years ago, the heavenly Father sent his Son. The Messiah arrived. He is Jesus Christ.

Now you have to establish that this historic person is truly the one expected for centuries. How do we know that Jesus is the Savior, the Redeemer?

Christ claimed to be God. He was accused of blasphemy. He said, "I and the Father are one." It was precisely on these charges that the people of his day clamored for his death. However, Jesus proved beyond a shadow of a doubt that he was God as well as man. He fulfilled all the expectations of Scripture, the biblical prophecies. Christ demonstrated his divinity by his miracles, especially his greatest miracle, his Resurrection, rising from the dead.

You can prove all this?

Yes. This is documented in the New Testament, the second half of the Bible relating to Christ, his life, and his teachings. The number and variety of Jesus' miraculous signs is overwhelming. The blind saw, the deaf heard, the lame walked, the mute spoke, the incurable lepers were instantaneously cleansed, and the dead were restored to life. Christ walked on the water, calmed stormy seas, and multiplied five loaves of bread and two fish to feed thousands. He predicted that he would go to Jerusalem, be betrayed, be executed, and on the third day rise from the tomb. Eyewitnesses testified to these happenings steadfastly, even to their own martyrdom.

Though this is impressive, what does it prove?

That Jesus is God! It proves that what he said is true.

How does Christ's life relate to me and to the rest of the world?

Relationship with God was severely damaged by original sin and by the personal sins of every person who walked on earth. Jesus offered himself on the cross to pay the price of our sin, to atone for our defiance and disobedience. He restored the loving relationship with the heavenly Father. He communicated this Good News, the Gospel, personally. That's why he is correctly called the First Evangelizer. Evangelization means bringing God's good news that real happiness is possible for everyone.

The five minutes are up. This has been a succinct explanation. The details of how men and women are to relate to God still have to be explained in this context. I'll give you ten seconds to wrap up your presentation.

Jesus said it this way: "I am the way, and the truth, and the life. No one comes to the Father except through me. If you know me, you will know my Father also. From now on you do know him and have seen him" (Jn 14:6–7).

How challenging is it to become a Christian?

It is possible for everyone to follow Christ. But just saying "Lord, Lord" is not enough. Faith and good works go hand in hand. Saint James said that faith without works is dead (2:17). That was the reason for the short prayer that began my explanation. Our lives have to conform to God's will. Notice that when Jesus said "repent and believe" the word *repent* came first. Faith is not merely an intellectual game. Becoming a Christian is the challenge of a lifetime and involves a lifetime of challenge.

Are you encouraging me or discouraging me?

Evangelization is invitational. Jesus said, "Come follow me." Christ defines the relationship. And the relationship is defined by love. "No one has greater love than this, to lay down one's life for one's friends" (Jn 15:12).

Something Extra

Do Catholics read the Bible?

Yes. They consider the Bible to be the inspired word of God by which he revealed to the Jewish and early Christian people who he is and how they can attain salvation.

The Bible is made up of many shorter works collected together. The books of the Bible were written at different times and by different people.

There are two parts to the Bible: the Old Testament and the New Testament. The Old Testament talks about God's relations with the Jewish people before the coming of Jesus. The Old Testament consists of the first five books which are sometimes called the Pentateuch; the histories, which tell about the conquest of the Holy Land; the prophets, which record the words of those sent to Israel to call it back to the true belief in God; the writings, containing sacred songs (the psalms), advice on everyday living, and other explorations of religious issues. In the Greek tradition, which Catholics follow, the Old Testament contains forty-six books.

The New Testament, a collection of twenty-seven shorter books, talks about Jesus and his followers. It consists of the following: the Gospels, which are about Jesus' life on earth, his death, and Resurrection; letters, which were written to newly established communities to guide them in their faith; the Acts of the Apostles, which is a history of the activities of the early Church; and a book of prophesy, called Revelation.

CHAPTER THREE

Compelling Reasons

How do you get people to listen to you?

A percentage of folks are interested. Recall Christ's story about sowing seeds. Only some fell on fertile ground. If people's hearts are in the right place, they will be receptive.

You can also count on God's grace to help you deliver the Good News.

You told the story of Christ, tracing God's plan from Adam and Eve through the Old Testament books. The New Testament books related Christ's life and philosophy. How is the complete picture conveyed to prospective believers?

The apostles went out and said, "We have some great news for you!" They communicated in Judea and in Samaria, and all around the Mediterranean basin.

They visited towns and villages and cities. They entered homes and synagogues, speaking to gatherings and to individuals. They addressed Jews and Gentiles. People looked at them and asked, "What great news?" Peter and Andrew and James and the others declared, "The Savior of the world has arrived!" Folks responded, "We don't know what you are talking about." So Christ's communicators began to explain.

The Jews had the background of the Old Testament. There was something to build on when the disciples were talking to them. On the other hand, the Gentiles presented a series of challenges. They were pagans. Some believed in Greek gods, others in Roman gods. A wide variety of philosophies were prevalent. Saint Paul even encountered devotion to the Unknown God.

How did the apostles confront the challenges?

They explained how Mary was visited by the angel Gabriel, how she conceived through the power of the Holy Spirit, how Jesus was born in Bethlehem. They related how Christ lived his life, fulfilled the ancient prophecies, performed miracles and taught a sublime doctrine. This was done face to face, out loud, orally. Only after many years were their words written down. You and I know them today as the gospels of Matthew, Mark, Luke, and John. Evidently their words found receptive hearts because the number of Christians grew. The known world then was dominated and ruled by the Romans. It was a hostile environment for the apostles' message, but, even so, listeners found the gospels compelling.

Why did they find the gospels compelling? Were they regarded as a means to throw off Roman rule, to motivate rebellion?

Not at all! Christ's teaching is exclusively nonviolent. He said: "Peace I leave with you; my peace I give you....Do not let your hearts be troubled" (Jn 14:27).

Even so, becoming Christian was hazardous to the health of the early converts. What's the secret for attracting people even under these circumstances?

Christ did not promise heaven on earth, even though today folks still cling to that possibility. When they do, they are heading in the wrong direction, nourishing false hopes. Jesus said that those who wished to be his followers had to take up their crosses daily. He declared that those persecuted because of their faith in him were blessed. His teachings are clearly countercultural. He related a parable about a seed. Unless the seed is buried and dies, it does not bear fruit. Christianity is a paradox to those looking in from the outside.

So why did the movement catch on? Modern public relations firms would never recommend this approach. They would attempt to paint rosy pictures and build hopes for success.

The early Christians, as well as those who embrace Christ today, recognize the Gospel as the greatest love story ever told. Not only that, but it is all true. The coming of Christ is the world's most joyful event. They see the epitome of God's love in his Son. Jesus suffered torture, insult, and rejection out of love for every living person. He carried his cross to the height of Calvary. He offered the last drop of his precious blood in reparation for everyone's sins. This divine Person, true God and true man, sacrificed himself on the cross so that eternity and happiness would be available for every man, woman, and child. Jesus testified to the truth of God's love. Miraculously, Jesus rose from the dead, walked away from the tomb. He presents overwhelmingly convincing testimony.

So love is the answer? Love conquers? Love overcomes all obstacles?

The human heart responds to love. A lover conquers all adversaries. When people are evangelized, they come face to face with the sweetest music. Their spirits are lifted. They are convinced that God loves them. Their lives change. There is a transforming effect. "All the world loves a lover" says the lyrics of a song. No one has greater love than God. No one has greater love for each individual than Jesus Christ.

You make a good case. It seems that there ought to be more Christians intent on spreading the message. Not everyone has your enthusiasm, do they?

Lack of enthusiasm is a great barrier to evangelization. "It is manifested in fatigue, disenchantment, compromise, lack of interest, and a lack of joy and hope. We exhort all those who have the task of evangelizing, by whatever title and at whatever level, always to nourish spiritual fervor" (*A Summary: On Evangelization in the Modern World*, §80).

Are you confident that this can be done? That this evangelization effort is not a losing cause?

Jesus does not ask his apostles and followers to accomplish the impossible. This kind of a request would be unreasonable. We can point to history which shows communicating God's Good News has been successful; however Christ still must enlist the help of his followers. This is the way it is to be done. Christians are instruments of God's grace. There are many elements in the effort.

So Christ is looking for zealous, enthusiastic evangelizers?

Absolutely! But be mindful that this is a tandem enterprise, men and women working hand in hand with God, attempting to bear witness to their faith in Christ, and attempting to be the best communicators possible.

This zeal and enthusiasm are gifts of the Holy Spirit. As Pope Paul VI says: "The Holy Spirit is the principal agent of evangelization. It is he who inspires each individual to proclaim the Gospel, and it is he who causes the word of salvation to be understood and accepted. It was not by chance that the inauguration of evangelization took place on the morning of Pentecost under the inspiration of the Spirit" (*A Summary: On Evangelization in the Modern World*, §75).

Why do you think God uses men and women in evangelization? If God wishes to communicate, he can do this simply by willing it, can't he?

God does not make mistakes. He employs human beings in evangelization because this is the best way. There is great plausibility in one person speaking to another as an equal. Jesus became human not only to represent sinful humans, but to speak to humans in language they can comprehend. The message, in one sense, becomes more believable. The playing field is leveled.

What is the most compelling reason for becoming a Christian, a follower of Christ?

Jesus promises the ultimate prize, everlasting life. This is the goal. He says: "I am the resurrection and the life. Those who believe in me, even though they die, will live, and everyone who lives and believes in me will never die" (Jn 11:25-26).

You feel that Christ has given the key and the explanation of existence itself? Life has no real meaning without Christ? Is that what you're saying?

Saint Paul has a way with words. He says: "For to me, living is Christ and dying is gain" (Phil 1:21). If an evangelizer is in love with Christ and convinced of his belief, he knows there is no Plan B for this world. "Come and go with me to my Father's house where there's joy! joy! joy!" are the lyrics of a church hymn. There are sincere people searching for God, searching for meaning in their lives. They find fulfillment in Christ. Saint Augustine experienced great uneasiness in his life. He reminds us: "Our souls are restless, O Lord, and they will not rest until they rest in thee."

Something Extra

What is a parish?

Parishes are not shrines or lodges, exclusive communities, or clubs. A parish is a faith community that is challenged to involve everyone entrusted to them and include them as part of their membership. A parish is a community gathered and formed in order to celebrate the Eucharist. Another way to define a parish is through Canon law (the legal code under which the Catholic Church is governed). Canon 515 calls a parish "a certain community of Christ's faithful stabley established" within a diocese. The notion of parish is, therefore, composed of three strands:

1. It is an established community.
2. It receives its identity from its connection to the larger Church.
3. It is a community of believers.

That is why a parish embraces all of Christ's faithful in a defined area.

CHAPTER FOUR

Speaking for Christ

Many people are not comfortable speaking for Christ. They feel they do not know enough to evangelize. They feel that religion is more of a personal thing between God and themselves. If I suddenly started to evangelize, I fear my friends would think I have become a religious nut. How do you answer that?

Sharing faith in Christ has to flow naturally, from the heart. The individual's convictions are not wrenched from within unwillingly. In a way, men and women speak from experience, how their relationship with God is a comfort, a strength, and a joy. Remember that Peter and Andrew and James and the other apostles were eyewitnesses to Jesus' life, his death, and Resurrection. They heard his words. Once Jesus asked them if they wanted to go away. Peter spoke up and said, "Lord, to whom can we go? You have the words of eternal life" (Jn 6:68). His followers knew that Christ was united with the heavenly Father.

It does help the story to know that it comes from someone who has "been there." There is no substitute for firsthand experience. But that limits the numbers of potential evangelizers. My guess is that the majority of Christians do not practice their faith regularly. They do not worship the Lord on the Lord's Day faithfully, for example. How do you respond to that?

The apostles had an advantage. They were companions to Christ during his three years of public ministry. They saw and heard him. Miracles happened before their eyes. Being eyewitnesses was important for their credibility. Still they were aided and abetted by the Holy Spirit. When they considered a replacement for Judas, who betrayed Jesus and then hanged himself, the apostles sought another eyewitness. They chose Matthias. Mark, a gospel writer, was a companion to Peter. Luke, was Paul's companion. These evangelists heard the Good News firsthand.

I can see how people in the years immediately after Christ were impressed with the apostles. They were "for real." The integrity of their lives matched the words that they preached.

They were human beings and did not pretend to be otherwise. Once Paul and his companions were mistakenly called "gods" by the Lycaonians (Acts 14:11). He quickly pointed out that he was just like them. Peter, denied knowing Jesus when confronted in the courtyard of the high priest, Caiphas. He acknowledged his error and pledged his love for Christ threefold. Jesus did not require university graduates to communicate the kingdom of God. They learned from him walking the dusty roads of Palestine.

You seem to be making a point that almost anybody can evangelize. Is that so?

Not anybody! Those who believe in Christ! Evangelizers are instruments of God's grace. They wish to lead others to a belief in Christ that they enjoy. But almost everybody with faith can and should encourage. No one should underestimate their influence when they are hand in hand with God.

What about circumstances when Christians devoutly wish those close to them to be followers of Christ? Even so, there is hesitation. They do not want sweethearts or spouses to become Christian simply because of them and their faith.

They should be straightforward. Tell fiancés, husbands, and wives how strongly their faith is centered in Christ. Make no secret that they are praying for them. Explain that a choice to become a Christian has to be based on a love of Christ himself. Becoming a Christian is not simply a matter of "getting religion" to please the ones they love. The merits of following Christ speak for themselves. The motivation for conversion has to be true. It has to be genuine. Faithful Christians who devotedly practice their faith are themselves occasions of grace. "You will receive power when the Holy Spirit has come upon you; and you will be my witnesses in Jerusalem, in all Judea and Samaria, and to the ends of the earth" (Acts 1:8).

Churchgoers are likely to have people ask them about attending and belonging. Others, who do not frequent faith communities, may be curious, even a little envious. They may sense that there is something missing in their lives. How does an evangelizer handle these inquiries?

Parishioners would do well to invite those who show interest in learning more about their faith community. They should make inquirers feel welcome. They should share the rationale of practicing the faith and participating in the life of the Church.

One way to do this is to answer their questions candidly and follow up with more information as necessary.

So there should be great effort to invite outsiders. Are parishioners encouraged to reach out? This outreach does not appear to be a prominent effort in many Catholic churches?

There ought to be clear signs of parishioners interested in the spiritual life of others. They are not to say, "I've got mine. You get yours." This is contrary to Christ's spirit. Saint Paul says: "If you do not have the spirit of Christ, you do not belong to Christ." Evangelization is the essential mission of the Church. The reason why it is the Church's essential mission is because it is Christ's essential mission. Christians must participate in Christ's mission.

Parishioners are probably more comfortable inviting their friends and neighbors to church than they are talking about Jesus Christ. How do you answer that?

There is nothing wrong about inviting people to church. It is a good idea. "Open Wide the Doors to Christ" is a millennium-year slogan. Those invited deserve to have the prayers and songs and liturgy explained so they will understand how God is being worshiped. Invitation is a stepping-stone to evangelization, coming to know, and hopefully, coming to love, Jesus Christ.

What about the sermon, the homily?

That, too, merits explanation. As a general rule, the preaching flows from the Scripture readings which are proclaimed. Selections from the Old Testament, the New Testament, and, particularly, the gospel, set the theme for the Sunday liturgy. Visitors are enlightened by God's own word. The Church calendar celebrates the life and teachings of Jesus, from his birth, Christmas, to his death and Resurrection on Easter. Churchgoers have the benefit of spiritual nourishment from week to week.

So this a great challenge for the ordinary churchgoer?

Not really. Many parishes have religious calendars. Religious congregations and missionary orders offer complimentary calendars, too. A parishioner will be able to point out the seasons of Advent, Christmas, Easter, Pentecost, and the other timely celebrations of the Church. Saints' days are usually featured on these calendars as well. Those interested in the faith will welcome this information that serves to guide and give direction to a person's yearly faith journey.

Experiencing church for the first time is unique. There must be millions who do not know what it is like to enter the building. They probably have a mountain of questions. How do you deal with these?

One way to allay the fears of inquirers is to pick a quiet time and take them on a tour of a church building. You should be aware that there are pamphlets explaining churches and their furnishings put out by many different organizations. Some offer little booklets that outline the major aspects of a church building. Some parishes might even sponsor special events so that non-churchgoers can become acquainted. The challenge of sharing one's faith and its practice is not difficult and can soon become second-nature to those who are dedicated on its behalf. The altar, the reconciliation rooms (confessionals), the tabernacle, the sanctuary lamp, the Stations of the Cross, all are objects of interest that assist the faithful in relating to God.

Care should be made not to show off the premises just to satisfy curiosity. The church is the house of God. There are churches in virtually every land that are offered as tourist attractions and museums, but that is not the purpose of these activities. The sincere of heart who are seeking God want to know why parishioners worship as they do.

Are you are saying that relationship with the heavenly Father does not happen in a vacuum, that individuals are not really left on their own to climb the mountain of the Lord.

God has communicated. Evangelizers assist in explaining and demonstrating how the faith is embodied in time and in place. Christ lives among us.

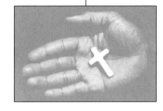

Something Extra

***What is faith? It sounds so vague to me.
Can you explain?***

Faith is more than just the facts about Jesus. It is an attitude of mind and heart by which we trust in a loving God who will care for us no matter what we have done.

Faith is a gift from God. It transforms us into believers in the truth and meaning of salvation. Faith admits us into the community of the Lord, the family of Jesus, who are all joined to one another and to him in faith.

CHAPTER FIVE

Little Things

It seems to me that there must be a lot of small things that the unskilled evangelizer can do. My guess is that most Christians feel inadequate, even uncomfortable sharing their faith. What is your experience?

Little things mean a lot in the evangelizing effort. Collectively, Christians practicing their faith are powerfully influential. They represent the Church individually and as a faith-filled community. "You are the Church," the late Cardinal Cushing of Boston declared with ringing tones. "It is therefore primarily by the Church's conduct, by living witness of fidelity to the Lord Jesus that the Church will evangelize the world" (*A Summary: On Evangelization in the Modern World*, §41).

Suggest things to do. What can the man and the woman in the church pews do to further the cause?

The Bible uses the word *witness* more than one hundred times, and the word *witnesses* forty times in various contexts and meanings. "With great power the apostles gave their testimony to the resurrection of the Lord Jesus, and great grace was upon them all" (Acts 4:33). There is no difficulty listing things to do. However it should be clear to those who wish to help in evangelizing that there has to be conscientious witness to Jesus himself as the basis for these actions.

What can we do?

1. Be faithful and consistent worshiping the Lord on the Lord's Day, participating in the sacrifice of the Mass.

2. Visit Christ, who is truly present in the Blessed Sacrament, the tabernacle, during the week. Spend personal, quiet time in prayer.

3. Pray privately and publicly, for example, make the Sign of the Cross, and say grace before meals at home and in restaurants.

4. Be active in your parish as a lector, a eucharistic minister, a religious education teacher, altar server, parish council member, and in other capacities.

5. Wear religious medals, crucifixes, Christian symbols, and so on.

6. Place objects of devotion on the desk at home, at work (if allowed). Display pictures of Christ and the saints, plaques.

7. Make it known that you are a practicing Catholic, one who believes in Christ, and are available to assist others by answering questions, by uniting in prayer.

8. Offer to pray with those who tell you their troubles. Perhaps they suffer anxieties because of illness, or they are sad at the loss of a loved one.

9. Attend wakes and funerals of neighbors, parishioners, and relatives. Offer sympathy to the living. Pray for the departed souls.

10. Actively support your children's punctual and regular attendance at Mass. Coordinate their worship with their religious education classes. Make sure they know the importance of each. Remind them that at class they study about Jesus, and at Mass, they unite with him.

11. Display shrines outdoors: statues, crucifixes, Christmas Nativity scenes, and so on.

12. Be a volunteer for the parish door-to-door census or visitation.

13. Observe the liturgical seasons and feasts at home with prayers and customs. Along with birthdays, celebrate the baptismal names of family members according to their saints' days.

14. Participate in retreats, Cursillos (a renewal program), charismatic gatherings, conferences, prayer sessions, and so on. Be mutually supportive and encouraging.

15. Subscribe to Catholic publications. Read them regularly: newspapers, magazines, periodicals, and so on. Share the publications with others after you have read them, for example: neighbors, prisoners, patients in hospitals, among other places.

16. Receive at least one mission magazine. Lend some financial support to a mission. Pray for missionaries and for the people they serve.

17. Review the meaning and significance of your baptism. See that it has to do with your ongoing personal conversion and commitment to Jesus Christ. Explain this to your children.

18. Kiss the crucifix each evening before retiring.

19. Read one of the gospels. Appreciate Christ and his teachings, his example and his sacrifice. See that this is, indeed, the greatest love story the world has ever known.

20. Tell the story of Christ in your own words: his conception, birth, life, miracles, torture, death, Resurrection, and establishing his Church. Practice with your children. Explain how your faith in Christ sustains you, and that Christ is your reason for living, your raison d'être.

21. When there is a death in the family of parishioners, ask if you can help. Does the parish have a special ministry to the bereaved?

22. Avoid occasions which are clearly and blatantly contrary to God's holy will, for example, pornography, fraud, hatred, racial prejudice, and so on.

23. Be generous with your God-given time, talent, and treasure. Cooperate with other parishioners. Consider tithing, that is, percentage-giving to your parish according to the biblical ideal.

24. Know your faith so that you can accurately answer questions about baptism, marriage, annulments, and so on.

25. Be active in pro-life causes. Do everything that is moral and legal to reverse policies and legislation that tolerate abortion, euthanasia, infanticide, and the death penalty.

26. Live the life of Christ. Maintain the spirit of Christ. Love your enemies. Do good to

those who harm you and hate you. Forgive those who sin (trespass) against you. Always return good for evil. Pray for those who hurt you.

27. When traveling, anticipate Sunday Mass schedules and the availability of parish churches. Visit shrines and places of pilgrimage.

28. In Bible reading, seek the correct interpretation of God's word as expressed by Christ's Church. Jesus established his Church for our guidance and direction.

29. Be respectful of those who profess other faiths and belong to other denominations. Read the documents of Vatican II regarding ecumenical relations with other Christians and non-Christians.

30. Pray for Christian unity, especially during the Week of Prayer for Christian Unity, January 18-25. Participate in ecumenical activities and devotions approved by the Church.

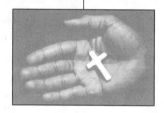

Something Extra

What are the goals of Catholic evangelization?

T he U.S. bishops, in their document *Go and Make Disciples:
A National Plan and Strategy for Catholic Evangelization
in the United States,* lists three goals addressed to every Catholic:

Goal I: To bring about in all Catholics such an enthusiasm for
their faith that, in living their faith in Jesus, they freely share it
with others. This goal is supported by these objectives:

- To foster an experience of conversion and renewal in
  each individual and parish
- To foster a greater appreciation of God's word in our
  lives
- To highlight the evangelizing dimension of the sacra-
  ments, especially the Sunday Eucharist
- To develop a deeper life of prayer among Catholics
- To instill a renewed understanding of the faith among
  Catholics
- To foster a greater sense of our homes as domestic
  churches
- To develop a spirituality for the workplace

Goal II: To invite all people in the United States, whatever their
social or cultural background, to hear the message of salvation
in Jesus Christ so they may come to join us in the fullness of the
Catholic faith. This goal is supported by the following objectives:

- To make every Catholic institution more welcoming
- To help every Catholic feel comfortable about sharing
  his or her faith

- To develop within families and households the capacity to share the Gospel
- To train Catholics to be evangelizers
- To use special family and parish times to invite people to faith
- To form a core of people to serve as ministers of evangelization
- To design programs that reach out in particular ways to those who have no church and to those who seek the fullness of faith
- To effectively welcome back those who have left the church

Goal III: To foster Gospel values in our society, promoting the dignity of the human person, the importance of the family, and the common good of our society, so that our nation may continue to be transformed by the saving power of Jesus Christ. This goal is supported by these objectives:

- To involve parishes and local service groups in alleviating the immediate needs of people in their areas
- To foster the importance of the family
- To explore issues of our workplaces and lay spirituality
- To encourage Catholic witness in the arts and intellectual community
- To involve Catholics in every level in areas of public policy, in the media, and in the questions of economic systems

CHAPTER SIX

Invitation to Follow

In the last chapter, you gave a list of practical suggestions for Christians to give witness to their faith. Presumably there comes a moment when the evangelizer offers a direct invitation to follow Christ. Is that so?

Yes. Non-Christians, those looking in from the outside, realize their lives are different from the lives of Christians. The faith element is missing. When the right moment arrives, it would be appropriate to invite non-Christians to share in the faith.

How would you do that?

Ask outright! Chances are that genuine interest already exists, especially if those inquiring have no faith community of their own. The conversation begins. It is informative. There is encouragement to pray, to ask for God's guidance and grace.

How would parishioners extend the invitation to family members, friends, and neighbors?

One way is to have a brochure available. The brochure could, for example, have an attractive graphic of Jesus Christ embracing the world. It might ask "Would you like to become a Catholic?" Inside is helpful information (an example of the content of such a brochure is found on page 155).

The Good-News giver might start with such information as the following: The word *catholic* derives from a Greek word which means "universal." Jesus came to save everyone. After his resurrection from the dead, Jesus commissioned his apostles. "Go therefore and make disciples of all nations, baptizing them in the name of the Father and of the Son and of the Holy Spirit, and teaching them to obey everything that I have commanded you" (Mt 28:19–20). They were to bring the "Good News" of God's love to every person. In A.D. 110, Saint Ignatius, Bishop of Antioch, declared, "Where Jesus Christ is, there is the Catholic Church." Saint Ignatius succeeded Saint Peter, apostle and first pope, as the bishop in Antioch. From Antioch, Saint Peter then went on to Rome.

The message gives significant information about Christ, the apostles, and the Church, and also offers other helpful information and encouragement.

So you are in the communication business, aren't you?

Yes, religion cannot be understood except in terms of communication and connectedness. God communicates to his people. His greatest communication is sending his Son, Jesus Christ, to save us.

Communicate and convert! Is that the idea?

Not exactly! Close, but no cigar! Information is proliferated on radio, television, film, press, and computer. The Internet is a gigantic encyclopedia. All these modern means of communication are blessings. Evangelization is not just communication. It calls for something more. The Church says this: "Communication is more than the expression of ideas and the indication of emotion. At its most profound level, it is the giving of self in love. Christ's communication was, in fact, spirit and life" (*Communio et Progressio*, "Pastoral Instruction on the Means of Social Communication," §11).

So pamphlets and books and other informational items will not do the trick by themselves.

They can be very helpful, but God's communication always sends love. And truth, too. Those seeking God need to be reached. They also have to accept the notion that religion isn't up for grabs. It isn't just another fad or passing fancy. They need to realize that God communicates clearly and accurately. They need to pray, and they need to be prayed for. The more ideal the conditions are, the more conducive the climate is to effective communication and conversion.

The modern means of communication, radio, TV, film, the Internet dominate the thoughts of most men and women. The "God element" is minimized. The expression of religion seems to be tolerated rather than influencing every phase of human activity. That makes for a difficult job, doesn't it?

The evangelizer does well to pray "Thy kingdom come." Jesus sent his followers and told them to declare "the kingdom of heaven has come near" (Mt 10:7). In effect, they were encouraged to proclaim that this is God's world. But if God and religion are left out, if there is little or no reference to him, the human mind is set in other directions.

So that is what they mean when they say "secularism"?

Yes. Webster's dictionary says that secularism "rejects any form of religious faith and worship."

Secularism presents a real challenge, doesn't it?

Jesus says, "Everyone therefore who acknowledges me before others, I will also acknowledge before my Father in heaven; but whoever denies me before oth-

ers, I will also deny before my Father in heaven" (Mt 10:32). Pope John Paul II in his apostolic letter on the third millennium, *Tertio Millennio Adveniente*, calls for a commitment to meet the challenge of secularism. "It will be fitting to broach the vast subject of the crisis of civilization, which has become apparent especially in the West, which is highly developed from the standpoint of technology but is interiorly impoverished by its tendency to forget God or to keep him at a distance. The crisis of civilization must be countered by the civilization of love, founded on the universal values of peace, solidarity, justice, and liberty, which find their full attainment in Christ" (§52).

The tendency of our modern civilization to keep God at arm's length presents something of a problem, doesn't it?

Communicating Christ has always been a challenge. That difficulty, in itself, is a sad commentary on the human condition. We need to recall that Jesus was perfect in every way. He is the Son of God. But Christ was rejected, crucified.

So there is no giving up?

There can be no giving up on Christ and his essential mission.

Christians were deprived of their civil rights, exiled and martyred during the first three centuries of Christianity. The challenge takes on different forms as time goes by, doesn't it?

Saint Paul in his second letter to the people of Corinth indicates his determination as an evangelizer. He encourages them not to receive the grace of God in vain. "We are putting no obstacle in anyone's way, so that no fault may be found with our ministry, but as servants of God we have commended ourselves in every way: through great endurance, in afflictions, hardships, calamities, beatings, imprisonments, riots, labors, sleepless nights, hunger; by purity, knowledge, patience, kindness, holiness of spirit, genuine love, truthful speech, and the power of God; with the weapons of righteousness for the right hand and for the left; in honor and dishonor, in ill repute and good repute. We are treated as impostors, and yet are true; as unknown, and yet are well known; as dying, and see—we are alive; as punished, and yet not killed; as sorrowful, yet always rejoicing; as poor, yet making many rich; as having nothing, and yet possessing everything" (2 Cor 6:3–10).

Something Extra

What are some ways to reach out to others as an evangelizer?

1. Train yourself to be a good listener. Listen with your heart, your mind, and your ears. Make a commitment to concentrate carefully on what others are saying. Give complete attention to the speaker rather than rushing to frame a response before the other person has finished speaking. Try to grasp the real meaning of the other person's words. Also pay close attention to nonverbal cues: posture, facial expression, eye contact, tone of voice, and so on. Train yourself to understand and acknowledge the beliefs of the other person.

2. Ask respectful and sincere questions about what people are saying and how they feel. These kinds of questions keep the dialogue going. If you decide to ask questions, commit yourself to listening to the answer without interruption.

3. Don't let the dialogue go on too long before bringing up the topic of God and faith. Many people just naturally shy away from discussing religious matters and its meaning to them. In approaching this subject, though, select a suitable point to insert it in the conversation. Warm up your listener; don't just begin without laying the groundwork.

4. Rehearse your story of the Good News of salvation so that you can communicate it in a concise way suitable to the needs of the listener. Lots of people are more comfortable talking about their favorite saint or the Catholic view on economic justice than they are in discussing how Christ became incarnate in order to die for our sins.

5. Make your story interesting and lively. Use personal experi-
    ence, items from recent news events, parables from the New
    Testament, or quotations from the popes, the saints, or the
    doctors of the Church to get your points across. As you "tell
    the Good News," keep the major ideas foremost: sin and sal-
    vation, freedom and commitment, faith and love.

6. Make your statements about Jesus Christ in an ordinary and
    down-to-earth way. This is not hocus-pocus, but our real fu-
    ture. As a matter of social propiety, many people are loathe
    to discuss the issue of where God fits into their lives, but if
    someone else brings it up they become eager to talk about
    it. Be sure to follow-up your conversation by sending more
    information or inviting people to coffee or church meetings
    or discussion clubs.

CHAPTER SEVEN

Why Become a Christian?

What do you say to people who tell you they are not interested in religion?

Never force the conversation if people want to avoid the subject. They may become even more adamant in their disclaimer of interest. The situation becomes strained, perhaps unpleasant. If they want to explain why they are opposed, what are the underlying reasons for their aversion, that may be a starting point for a continued conversation.

So, a good evangelizer must know enough not to pursue a particular line of discussion?

That's true. Jesus once sent his disciples into towns and villages. If the inhabitants were unwilling to listen, he advised his disciples to leave, to shake the dust from their feet, to begin again in another area.

Some people know a little bit about religion. Some know more. Some claim unpleasant experiences. How do evangelizers handle this distrust of religion?

Some may even feel superior to religious people on account of their avoidance of religious practices altogether. The irreligious may ridicule and downgrade churchgoers. So what else is new? They ridiculed and crucified Jesus, too. However some irreligious people may just protest too much. Unwittingly, their protests may signal the despair of their lack of relationship with God. This dispair may manifest itself in subtle ways but also in vocal denials. Psychologically speaking, something is missing from their lives.

What would you do? Try again some other day?

Pray for them. Ask God to send them his grace. Estimate each occasion. Let them know if they ever want to talk about it in the future, you are available.

Let's say there is some interest. Any favorable approaches?

An evangelizer appreciates opportunities. He or she realizes there are grace-filled occasions. If there is true friendship, the disinterested party may just bring up the subject again.

Pretend I have raised the topic anew. What would you say?

God calls us all to a wonderful relationship with him. He has blessed us with life, with individuality, and with all the material things we enjoy. These have been entrusted to us. We have responsibilities to God. There is a judgment day coming.

You would talk about Judgment Day?

Why not? It is a reality. It is inevitable for everyone. If there is accountability for school lessons, for financial investments, for labor, there is nothing extraordinarily incongruous about rendering an account to God for all his gifts and blessings in life. Every individual has a report card. "For all of us must appear before the judgment seat of Christ, so that each may receive recompense for what has been done in the body, whether good or evil" (2 Cor 5:10).

Isn't this a bit scary?

The Bible is full of lines extolling the fear of the Lord as a suitable virtue. This fear is the beginning of wisdom. Just the start, of course. God hopes and expects us to mature into loving sons and daughters confident of his care for us.

There are some people who are not religiously inclined. They say, "I've been all right up until now. Why change?"

God calls us to a loving relationship with him. Life is only worth living if it is lived in harmony with God. No man is an island. The answer is God. Jesus shows the way. You might say they do not know what they are missing. But they will in time. Life is only meaningful if it is lived as the Creator intended.

What if people offer specific difficulties. Often well intentioned, hale and hearty souls say good-naturedly, we are all going to the same place (namely heaven). It doesn't make much difference how we get there. All religions are pretty much the same. If I mind my own business and I am kind to my neighbor, that should take care of things. How is this response handled?

There are men and women who lump religions into one generic "I'm all right, You're all right" category. And there are folks who are kind and caring seemingly by nature. This is something to build on. Remember that God calls us not to a natural destiny, but a supernatural destiny. Everlasting happiness in the next life is only possible through Jesus Christ.

You are not saying that everyone who is not a Christian, not a Catholic, is going to hell are you?

Of course not! But every person living on earth will only attain supernatural happiness through Christ. This goes for everyone, for every man, woman, and child, of all races, colors, and creeds. It may be that some will never have heard of God's great love, that the heavenly Father sent his Son. Nevertheless, according to the graces that they receive in life, according to their sincere response, they are to respond lovingly to the love God has given. It is what theologians call a baptism of desire. Whether they come to the knowledge of Christ or not, their eternal salvation is attained by virtue of Christ's sacrifice, death, and Resurrection.

How do we know if they have attained this baptism of desire?

We don't. We simply recognize that, through the beneficent mercy of God, it is possible. There is no listing of those who are in hell. There is no listing of those who are in purgatory. There is a partial listing of those who are in heaven. We call these people "saints."

So baptism is necessary for salvation?

Yes! Sacramentally, through water and the Holy Spirit. Also, through martyrdom, dying for Christ. This is called baptism of blood. Jesus said, "Very truly, I tell you, no one can enter the kingdom of God without being born of water and Spirit" (Jn 3:5).

There are those who say it really doesn't matter what a person believes. It is how you act that counts. How can that objection be answered?

There is a Latin expression, *Agere sequitur esse,* "To act follows to be!" We act according to character. Our actions follow our convictions. The human mind grasps truth, comprehends truth. Downplaying doctrine means downplaying truth. Downplaying dogmas means trivializing principles. We act according to our beliefs. It is very important to have principles grounded in truth. We esteem people of principle. They offer stability to society. To say it does not matter what a person believes is nonsense. There is an old saying: "One mistake in principle means a thousand mistakes in practice."

Give me an example.

Human life! God's gift of life is sacred. God expects us to respect human life. "Thou shalt not kill!" Dominion over life belongs exclusively to God. The laws of the land, for the most part, uphold an individual's right to live. Murder is a crime. Disregard the principle, and you trivialize human life. If a government makes a law that contradicts God's dominion and his commandments, it is a grave error. There are serious consequences to the detriment of society. God knows what works and what does not work. Christ guides us unswervingly to the heavenly Father. For all the above reasons and many more, becoming a Christian is a tremendous blessing. The Lord has not left us without direction and guidance.

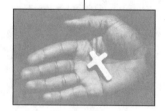

Something Extra

What are some of the barriers to being an evangelizing Catholic and how can they be overcome?

1. *I worry about being ridiculed.* This concern may very well arise from a notion that others will reject information about Jesus Christ. This fear may be underestimating the powerful attraction of the Good News. This worry may be based more on our own lack of confidence rather than the response of others. There are several ways for dealing with this concern. First, acknowledge this fear and then seek counsel and advice from someone who has overcome it. Second, remember that we are all given the fruits of the Holy Spirit, which can be used to help us offset negative emotions: joy, love, peace, patience, kindness, generosity, faithfulness, gentleness, and self-control. Third, remember the future—God works in mysterious ways and grace, though powerful, may take a long time to come to fruition.

2. *I don't "do" evangelization.* It's not my job—it belongs to the priests, the deacons, or the someone in an official capacity. It is helpful to remember that evangelization is more a matter of commitment rather than specialized competence. The Gospel forthrightly proclaims that a disciple must go out into the world and spread the Good News. Evangelization is the mission and purpose of the whole Church; it is the doing of God's will and work on earth.

3. *I don't have the foggiest notion how to evangelize.* Claiming this kind of ignorance really is an excuse. The skills used in evangelization are often identical to those that we use in our personal affairs or our business lives: listening skills, speaking skills, and organization and planning tools. But the most

important need in evangelization is a truly loving heart firmly dedicated to speading the message of Jesus Christ. This claimed ignorance may also be a cover-up for a lazy soul. Evangelization is a "doing" ministry. Jesus didn't stay at home, but rather traveled from place to place, preaching, teaching, and healing.

4. *I'm not a "good enough" Catholic.* Saying that you don't know the faith well enough to convince someone else is not an unsurmountdable obstacle. Certainly, a well-grounded knowledge can gradually be acquired by studying the great truths of Catholic Tradition and by carefully articulating one's own explanation for his or her faith. A study of the teachings of the Church not only enhances the mind and heart of the evangelizer but also develops a sense of unity with other Catholics in our own community. Extremely important on the faith journey is the use of the tools of praying and learning about Scripture. These tools are essential earmarks of a disciple.

These tools will give an essential grounding for evangelization. Other experiences, such as parish retreats with group discussion, parish groups with a focus on sharing experiences, and various renewal programs, will help even shy Catholics become more articulate about their faith.

CHAPTER EIGHT

Challenge

So is it difficult to become a Christian?

Well, it is more challenging than difficult.

How is it challenging? There are millions of Christians. Some do not seem to be overly challenged.

Some may not appear to be overly challenged. However, it may be that they simply do not recognize their call to perfection. They settle back into a routine life, only occasionally referring to their relationship with God. Jesus said, "Be perfect, therefore, as your heavenly Father is perfect" (Mt 5:48).

How does a person become perfect?

By following Jesus Christ, for he is "the way, the truth, and the life."

So is this possible? Can anyone actually follow in Christ's footsteps to perfection?

No one can become true God and true man like Jesus. But they can become the best they can be. Men and women can correspond to the graces given by God. They can attain a degree of perfection acceptable to God. Jesus defines the relationship. Study his words, and discover what he teaches. Focus on his life and dedication. Others have done this.

Then, it is not easy becoming a Christian. There are countless numbers who are not willing to go down a road that is difficult to travel. They are influenced by today's philosophy and by television commercials. There is constant search for the easy way out of all difficulties. Am I on the right track here?

It is true that some people seek the easy way out. But human beings are usually not satisfied with themselves unless they do their best. This explains why teachers in schools encourage their pupils to become the best students they possibly can be, and why coaches motivate baseball players and basketball players to rise above mediocrity, and why mothers and fathers want their sons and daughters to succeed in life and assist them in meeting challenges.

When I was growing up I heard some kids saying they would not want to be Catholic. They said Catholics have to go to church every Sunday. Apparently they felt life was better not having to make this commitment.

There are people who feel that it is burdensome to worship the Lord on the Lord's Day with regularity. Catholic practice conforms to the commandments. When God called Moses to the top of Mount Sinai and communicated his commandments, Moses understood very well that these were commandments, not options.

So it is a matter of neglect when we do not worship the Lord on Sundays?

This is all part of the perfection process. Slowly, gradually, the Lord forms our character. Through the expression of his holy will, he molds us in his image. Of course, it is serious neglect. If your mother or father directed you, and you ignored them, you act to your detriment. They love you, after all. Children are not to tell their parents what to do. They are called to respond lovingly. Their parents are acting on their behalf. They have their best interests at heart.

There seems to be a common thought that when someone dies, they automatically go to heaven. Is this idea realistic?

The idea that everyone gets an automatic ticket to heaven is really wishful thinking. It may mean that some people do not see the full implication of the Christian challenge.

Do they trivialize the quest for eternal happiness?

It is a kind of childlike perspective. Christians who have developed in maturity do not automatically locate departed souls in paradise. Folks are encouraged to read Christ's teachings. Jesus' Sermon on the Mount outlines the challenge of following him from day to day. "Enter through the narrow gate; for the gate is wide and the road is easy that leads to destruction, and there are many who take it. For the gate is narrow and the road is hard that leads to life, and there are few who find it" (Mt 7:13-14).

What about children? When a child dies, we say, almost instinctively, that he or she is in heaven with God.

When a baptized child passes away before attaining the use of reason, we consider that child to be with God. This is a common belief. The child has committed no personal sins. This state of affairs could be true also for unbaptized children. However we do not know the answer. God, in his mercy, may grant them his grace. There is nothing revealed about this in Scripture. God's ways are loving, but mysterious.

So if I decided to follow Christ, I would find the course demanding. This is not a Madison Avenue type of approach. Are there those who think about it, and then, walk away?

There was a young man who did this very thing. And you are right! Jesus did not entice people with politicians' promises. Jesus' invitations are not slick and not commercial.

What about the young man?

Saint Matthew's Gospel records an incident. The young man asks Jesus what he has to do to gain eternal life. Christ answers that he has to keep the commandments. Quite eagerly the youth says that he has kept God's commandments. What's lacking in my life? he inquires. "If you wish to be perfect, go, sell your possessions, and give the money to the poor, and you will have treasure in heaven; then come, follow me," Jesus tells him (Mt 19:21). The young fellow went away sad, because he had many possessions and couldn't bear to part with them.

It's not wrong to have possessions, is it?

No. We all have basic needs. Evidently the man was attached to his possessions. He was possessive to the extent that he could not give Jesus the total gift of himself. Perfection calls for a state of mind. This calls for loving God with our whole heart and soul. This is not new. Christians have probably heard this primary commandment for years but have never pondered the full impact of its meaning.

The Christian challenge is formidable. Is it possible for anyone to gain eternal life?

The disciples listening in on Jesus' conversation with the young man asked the same question. "Then who can be saved?" (Mt 19:25). Christ assured them that it was possible, but not without challenge. "For mortals it is impossible, but for God all things are possible" (Mt 19:26).

If a person decided to accept the challenge, to become a Christian, to become a Catholic, he would not have to be perfect from the start, would he?

Not at all. God does not demand perfection. We are all challenged to follow in his footsteps. To become the perfect Christian is the challenge of a lifetime, and a lifetime challenge.

But a person would have to leave his wicked ways behind him and cross over the bridge. Right?

You have lifted the lyrics of a song to describe the situation. Everyone who decides to follow Christ is called to repentance. John the Baptizer preached this along the Jordan River. Jesus echoed John when he sent his disciples out on a mission. Conversion to Christ calls for a conversion of heart—a change in behavior.

Something Extra

How does an adult become a member of the Catholic Church?

Adults receive the sacrament of baptism (if they have not already done so) in order to become full members of the Church. In 1978, the Church reintroduced the "catechumenate" for adults wishing to be baptized in the Catholic Church. The "catechumen" is to be prepared for baptism over a suitable period of time but enters into a more intense period of preparation at the beginning of Lent (the period of forty days before Easter). This rite is called the Rite of Christian Initiation of Adults. Each period in the faith development of a catechumen is marked by a special, public rite. These periods can be shown in the following way:

- *Rite of Entrance into the Catechumenate:* Period of evangelization and inquiry which is completed upon entrance into the catechumenate.
- *Rite of Election:* Development of the catechumens' spirituality through prayer, reflection on the Scriptures, study, discussion, and faith-sharing.
- *Rite of Initiation:* Preparation of catechumens for baptism, confirmation, and Eucharist, usually at the Easter vigil. This period is usually conducted during the time of Lent.
- *Period of continued maturing as a disciple and member of the parish and the Church.*

A baptized Christian of another faith is usually received into the Church after a period of spiritual and doctrinal preparation by the bishop or a priest appointed by him. In this ceremony, the person makes a profession of faith. The sacrament of baptism may not be repeated, and only if there is reasonable doubt as to the fact or validity of earlier baptism is baptism bestowed conditionally.

CHAPTER NINE

Advantages

The challenge to become a Christian sounds like turning a person inside out. There seems to be the need for an interior transformation. Doesn't that mean that men and women are battling themselves?

Yes, indeed, the process is an internal one. Jesus said, "If any want to become my followers, let them deny themselves and take up their cross and follow me" (Mt 16:24).

This mandate from Jesus means changing our thinking. In some ways, it must mean changing the directions of our lives. Is that a true observation?

Yes. Sacrifice, taking up one's cross, self-denial—all are characteristic of the pursuit of Christian perfection. We are following Christ, after all, and the road is not an easy one.

And this has a transforming effect?

In time, and with the grace of God. "So if anyone is in Christ, there is a new creation: everything old has passed away; see, everything has become new!" (2 Cor 5:17).

As an evangelizer, are there persuasive words that you offer? Many men and women may enjoy a challenge, but this one lasts a lifetime. Doesn't there have to be some advantages?

Into every life, a little rain must fall. Years ago, there was a cartoon character who always seemed to have a cloud following him. Christians are positive people because Christ is positive. Nevertheless, life is not a bowl of cherries. There are hardships. There is no better way to face difficulties than with faith in Jesus Christ. If believers accept Christ and his teachings, if they embrace his philosophy of living, they can cope.

Calamities are devastating. Earthquakes and hurricanes destroy homes and livelihoods. Sickness and disease steal loved ones from their families. Poverty deprives folks of basic necessities. How can God be the author of all these difficulties?

God does not wish misery on anyone. Confusion, chaos, sin, and lack of harmony—all were introduced through the initial disobedience of Adam and Eve. These negatives are inevitable for all peoples in all ages. How to cope with them is another matter. How to sail the ship of life through stormy seas is everyone's dilemma and everyone's lot in life.

And Christians are better able to deal with them than others?

Saint Matthew's Gospel tells of Jesus and his apostles crossing the Sea of Galilee. Waves swelled and crashed the side of their boat. Christ was sleeping despite the danger. Filled with fear, they "woke him up, saying, 'Lord, save us.' And Jesus replied, 'Why are you afraid, you of little faith?' Then he got up and rebuked the winds and the sea, and there was a dead calm" (Mt 8:26). Jesus can still the storms of Christians' lives.

Christ demonstrated divine power. You're not suggesting that every time there are desperate circumstances, when Christians pray, there will be a miracle, are you?

Certainly not. Christ experienced torture and death himself. In following Christ, his Christians have to carry their own crosses. But he demonstrates how to cope. He calls for faith and love.

Some people seem to abandon Christ if things do not go their way. They blame God for their misfortunes. What answer do you have for them?

The "blame game" is always a significant excuse. There is a little story about two prisoners looking out through the iron bars after a rain storm. One looked down and saw mud puddles. The other looked up and saw the stars. We can cope better if we look up.

Cute story! Will it float in real life?

In his book, *The Life God Blesses*, Gordon MacDonald, tells this story. A Chinese pastor, who was imprisoned for eighteen years, related his experience at a conference in England. People asked him how he maintained his health. He said life in prison was miserable. He was assigned to shovel out the human waste from the camp's cesspool. His atheistic captors delighted in assigning him to the task. He was well educated and a Christian leader. The stench was so revolting both guards and prisoners kept their distance. When the cesspool was filled, and ripe, the pastor had to walk in the waste, and empty it. But surprisingly, he said he enjoyed the task. Why? Because of the solitude, being alone with God, praying aloud for his needs, reciting the Scriptures he remembered, and psalms, too. He sang hymns, particularly favorites. And he imagined walking with Jesus, telling him that he was his own. The pastor experienced the Lord's presence under the most unpleasant circumstances. That good man had faith. He coped.

That is a good story—a powerful one, but isn't it a bit extreme?

Christians learn to meet the ordinary, daily challenges with faith. Rich and poor manage because they have faith. They do not walk alone. There is a real dependency on God. They acknowledge this dependency. This is the proper perspective. God is the only independent being. Humans are dependent on God for everything. Christians turn to God in prayer. They are in dialogue with God. They build a relationship.

I've heard it said that sometimes religious people have their heads in the clouds. They pay more attention to things of the next world and not enough for things of this world. What do you say to that?

I answer with Saint Paul's admonition: "So if you have been raised with Christ, seek the things that are above, where Christ is, seated at the right hand of God. Set your minds on things that are above, not on things that are on earth" (Col 3:1–2). It is possible to earn a living and be part of society as well as being a person of faith. Virtue lies in the middle. Some of our great saints were very active in this world. Their generosity and zeal was motivated by their love for God, and their faith in God.

How often should people pray?

As often as they like. The habit of prayer is a blessing and a grace. Generally speaking, Christians should pray morning and evening. Some folks tell us that they talk to God all day long—which certainly follows Jesus' admonition to "pray always and not to lose heart."

And God always answers?

Yes! In his own way, and in his own time. Jesus said, "Ask, and it will be given to you; search, and you will find; knock, and the door will be opened for you" (Mt 7:7). Our requests are conditioned by God's will: "Thy will be done."

You feel all this is an advantage, that men and women are better able to weather the storms of life if they are people of faith?

There is no doubt about it. Jesus teaches us how to pray. He himself prayed. Prayer is conversation with the heavenly Father. He loves us. Through prayer, our rapport with God is established and we are bonded to him.

Would evangelizers emphasize this?

Yes! They might share how consoling it is to pray, how prayer sustains them. Being able to pray is a great blessing. We do not walk alone. We may loose what is considered important, even precious. But God is with us. Emmanuel! The heavenly Father has sent his Son. We go to the Father through Jesus Christ.

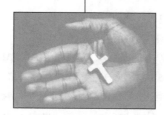

Something Extra

What are some fairly easy ways to evangelize?

1. Keep on your person a supply of attractive cards—if possible with an image of Christ on the front and an appropriate message on the reverse side. Distribute as you would business cards.

2. Participate in radio-talk shows, especially in those where a misunderstanding of Catholic beliefs is prevalent. Respond to these issues in a helpful manner; you may wish to write down your major points so that you can make a smooth presentation once your turn to speak arrives. You can usually speak on air under your first name, but often stations require a full name when calls are initially screened.

3. Display signs of your faith. Wear a cross or crucifix. Display religious pictures in your home. Put images of Jesus Christ in your automobile or in your wallet.

4. Write a letter to the editors of newspapers or magazines that misrepresent Catholic beliefs. Make your response brief and reasonable. To increase the possibility of getting your letter published, type your letter and include your name, address, and phone number so that the authenticity of the letter can be checked.

5. When you return books to the public library, leave invitational cards or leaflets as bookmarks in each volume.

6. Send faith-filled cards to people in celebration of life's events. Many religious bookstores and mail-order sources carry greeting cards with appropriate messages for birthdays, Easter, Christmas, Saint Patrick's Day, and so on.

7. Monitor on-line bulletin boards and chat rooms for opportunities to present Catholic beliefs in an accurate light. Train others to do likewise.

8. Volunteer to manage your parish's devotional library or pamphlet rack. Many parishes have lending libraries or for-sale literature displays in the church vestibule—or if your parish doesn't, volunteer to start them. Of course, the pastor or someone else knowledgeable may want to approve the kinds of materials included, but just concentrate on providing top-quality books and pamphlets that presents Catholic beliefs and practices in a straightforward and sensible way.

9. Share with others photocopies of relevant articles from Catholic sources—books, magazines, and newspapers. Permission from the publisher must be obtained and credit to the author and the source must be given, but this can usually be obtained via a phone call, e-mail, or letter.

10. Set up a system by which you pass on to others books on Catholic beliefs and issues. You may also wish to sponsor a book discussion so that recipients may share their opinions of what you have shared. To optimize this effort, you may wish to band together with other people to share costs, recycle books that you have already read, or scour secondhand bookstores to resurrect the Catholic classics.

11. Subscribe to Catholic periodicals and when you have finished reading them, leave them in the waiting rooms of hospitals, bus depots, train stations, as well as airline waiting areas.

12. Give gift subscriptions to Catholic periodicals as gifts.

CHAPTER TEN

Life After Death

The promise of life after death is powerfully persuasive. People have been talking about this idea for centuries. The Egyptians packed things in pyramids they thought would be helpful in the next life. There are various versions of what is supposed to happen after a person passes away. How does this concept fit into being Catholic?

Not all peoples and all races are accurate in their anticipation of the afterlife. However, Catholics believe that Jesus is the Son of God. His words about everlasting life are true and certain. By his own death and Resurrection, he verified his teachings. On the occasion of one of Christ's great miracles, raising his friend Lazarus from the dead after four days, he said, "I am the resurrection and the life. Those who believe in me, even though they die, will live, and everyone who lives and believes in me will never die" (Jn 11: 25-26).

So Christians have this expectation of eternal life because they believe in Christ?

Christ is always completely faithful to his promises. He, above all, keeps his word.

This belief has to be more than wishful thinking, doesn't it?

Following Christ is not merely an intellectual exercise. Christians must endorse Christ in their lives. Their faith calls for thoughts, words, and deeds—all according to the will of God. A belief in eternal life is much more than a pleasant idea. It is an article of faith— a reality of Christian existence.

What happens if they decide not to follow Christ? There were people who met Jesus face to face and walked away. They rejected his invitation to follow.

Faith is a gift from God. It is freely given to the sincere of heart. It is not the business of Christians to sit in judgment. Christ will come again to judge the living and the dead. Only God can fathom the human heart and comprehend a person's receptivity. It is good for us to remember that God loves each person with a tremendous love. Through baptism we become God's children.

You feel that God is more than fair in dealing with us?

True! Still there is a sense of urgency. It is difficult to interpret Christ's words without understanding the urgency that he himself communicated. "Go into all the world and proclaim the good news to the whole creation. The one who believes and is baptized will be saved; but the one who does not believe will be condemned" (Mk 16:15–16). Christ's mission of love is compelling. However, Catholics look at death in a different way than other Christian denominations.

How do you mean?

Catholics continue to pray for departed souls. Their funeral rites reflect a different approach than do non-Catholic services. Catholics believe that those who die in God's good graces are destined for eternal life. The faithful departed are not seriously sinful. But they may not be perfect in their love for God. They may have offended the all-loving God in lesser ways. These are not death-dealing sins, mortal sins. They are smaller sins. Catholic family members, parishioners, and friends pray and offer good deeds for the repose of their souls, for their eventual admission to eternal life.

Do you mean that departed souls can be helped? That there is a link, a connection, with them even after death?

"It is therefore a holy and wholesome thought to pray for the dead that they may be loosed from sins" (2 Macc 12:46—Confraternity Edition). The time-honored religious practice of praying for the dead goes back to the Old Testament. Many Catholics arrange to have Masses offered for their departed friends and relatives.

So after death, these people go to what you call purgatory?

Yes. Those who die in God's friendship undergo a purification in order to attain the holiness they need to enter God's presence. This truth flavors and colors the thinking of Catholics. The fact they can be effective in assisting the departed in their journey of faith is appealing. It is consoling. The departed suffer passively for their sins, certain that they will eventually enjoy heaven. At the same time, they are blessed by the intercession of their loved ones on earth.

So this a positive factor for evangelizers? Is their presentation of the gospel enhanced by this doctrine?

In the Church's official book for funeral rites it says, "We believe that all the ties of friendship and affection which knit us as one throughout our lives do not unravel with death." Also the funeral rite says: "May we who mourn be reunited one day with our brother (or sister); together may we meet Christ Jesus when he who is our life appears in glory." The words are compassionate. The religious practice is compelling.

Some say that funerals are for the living. What's your thought on this?

They can be inspirational for the living, as well as spiritually effective for the dead.

What do you think about eulogies where the lives of the departed are reviewed, and they are praised for their accomplishments?

Considered in the light of evangelization, eulogies can be helpful in praising God.

Evangelization means communicating the "Good News" of God's love—that the heavenly Father sent his Son, Jesus Christ, to live among us. If the eulogy of a person reflects God's love, this is a good thing. But Christ is always the center of our worship. At Mass Jesus Christ offers himself at the altar. At the conclusion of the eucharistic prayer, the consecrated Host and Precious Blood are held high, and Christ is proclaimed. "Through him, with him, and in him, in the unity of the Holy Spirit, all glory and honor is yours almighty Father, forever and ever." And then, in chorus, everyone sings, "Amen."

So Catholic funerals do not provide a stage to glorify human beings. Is this a good conclusion?

Yes. Recognition of holiness is a recognition of God's life within a person. To exemplify sanctity is a practice of the Church. Saint Paul says, "Think of us in this way, as servants of Christ and stewards of God's mysteries. Moreover, it is required of stewards that they be found trustworthy" (1 Cor 4:1-2). John the Baptizer, speaking of Christ, said, "He must increase, but I must decrease" (Jn 3:30).

So all this is appropriate for an evangelizer to talk about. Do you feel that this information about life after death is an attractive feature of Catholicism?

It is a necessary subject. Jesus spoke of everlasting life. If a person decided to follow Christ, this destiny would be part of the consideration. Heaven is mentioned hundreds of times in the Bible. When Jesus was being crucified, he promised paradise to the repentant thief. It is realistic to include life after death in conversation. God created human beings to share his own life. This is supernatural, that is, above the natural. How does a person get there from here? The answer is through Jesus Christ.

Everything hinges on Christ? There is no other way?

That is a wonderful and an accurate conclusion. A Christian's life is centered on Jesus Christ. He declared, "I am the way, and the truth, and the life. No one comes to the Father except through me" (Jn 14:6).

If someone truly believes this, the road to eternity is clearly charted, is it not?

"And without faith it is impossible to please God, for whoever would approach him must believe that he exists and that he rewards those who seek him" (Heb 11:6).

Something Extra

What are the questions that are frequently asked about the Catholic Church?

1. Why do Catholics confess their sins to a priest?
2. What must I do to be saved?
3. Why does the Catholic Bible have more books than the Protestant Bible?
4. Why do Catholics believe in a place between heaven and hell called "purgatory"? There's no place like that mentioned in the Bible.
5. Why do Catholics pray to Mary and the saints? Why not pray directly to God?
6. Why can't priests be married? Weren't some of the apostles married? Why does the Church insist on celibacy?
7. Why do Catholics believe that the Eucharist is the true body and blood of Christ?
8. Why do Catholics believe that the pope is infallible?
9. Why does the Catholic Church have so many dos and don'ts?
10. I'm divorced and remarried? Doesn't that automatically exclude me from the Church?
11. People like Moslems and Jews do not recognize Jesus. Do you mean to say that they will all go to hell?
12. What about birth control? Why is the Church so against it?

CHAPTER ELEVEN

The Eucharist

What is the most attractive feature of your faith in Christ? If I were considering becoming a Christian and a member of Christ's Church, what do you think would be most compelling?

Jesus Christ himself.

You mean just knowing about him and calling myself a follower?

The most attractive feature is being one with Jesus Christ, uniting with him. Jesus actually unites with us in his sacraments. He also unites with us through the Church, guiding us, directing us, consoling us, and encouraging us. Jesus calls us his friends. But beyond this wonderful relationship and also as part of this relationship, Jesus unites with us most significantly in the Eucharist.

You mean in holy Communion?

Yes. The Eucharist is a communication far beyond our expectations—a true communion with our God. Jesus decided to give us his greatest gift at the Last Supper on the night before he died. The Eucharist is a memorial, but more than that. Christ is truly, physically present, under the forms of bread and wine.

So when you receive holy Communion you believe that this is not merely a memorial?

Yes. This is perfectly clear. You can observe this in the conduct of Catholics. When they enter a church, they genuflect in front of the tabernacle where the Sacred Species are contained. This is a bow or a curtsy before the King of Kings. Notice the respect and reverence at the consecration of Mass, when the bread and wine are transubstantiated into the body and blood of Christ.

Other Christian denominations include a communion in their services. Is this communion just seen as a commemoration of Christ's presence? Are these generally considered only as memorials?

It is difficult to say how other Christian worshipers regard their communion services. There are over two hundred Protestant denominations in the United States. I think it is safe to say that some regard communion as a memorial of the Last Supper. Additionally, the Catholic Church teaches that it is necessary to have a valid priesthood to transubstantiate the elements of the bread and wine into the body and blood of Christ. Non-Catholic ministers do not regard themselves as priests and the Catholic Church does not recognize their ordination as relating to Christ's priesthood. The Eastern Orthodox, on the other hand, do trace the lineage of their priesthood to Christ.

So the Russian Orthodox and the Greek Orthodox and other Eastern Orthodox Christians have a valid priesthood, and Christ is physically present in their communion?

Yes, this is true. Pope John Paul II prays fervently for Christian unity, especially for reunion with the Eastern Orthodox churches.

How is it, then, that there is such divergence when it comes to so important a matter?

Catholics have always believed in our Lord's true presence in the Eucharist. The Acts of the Apostles speaks of "the breaking of the bread and the prayers" (Acts 2:42). Saint Justin wrote to the pagan Emperor Antonius Pius about A.D. 155 explaining Christian worship. The Council of Trent in the mid 1500s stated, "Because Christ our Redeemer said that it was truly his body that he was offering under the species of bread, it has always been the conviction of the Church of God...." During the Reformation years, the 1500s and 1600s, many divisions were created among Christians, consequently many divergent views.

How would you explain Christ's Real Presence in the Eucharist from the words of the Bible?

After one of Jesus' tremendous miracles, the feeding of thousands by multiplying five loaves of bread and a few fish, there was a showdown on the mountain. Crowds followed Jesus. Their stomachs were full and their eyes were wide with wonder. Jesus had given them a basis for belief, a foundation for their faith. However, some failed to make the connection. Jesus chastised them for following him only because they wanted more to eat. He declared, "I am the living bread that came down from heaven. Whoever eats of this bread will live forever; and the bread that I will give for the life of the world is my flesh" (Jn 6:51). They knew that he was speaking literally. Some walked away. They would no longer be his followers. They did not believe in Jesus and so they did not believe in his words. Still Jesus emphasized: "Very truly, I tell you, unless you eat the flesh of the Son of Man and drink his blood, you have no life in you" (Jn 6:53). Jesus was promising his greatest gift. And then, on the night before he died, at the Last Supper, at the first Mass, he took the bread and said, "This is my body." He took a cup of wine, and said, "This is the cup of my blood."

So, do you feel that receiving Christ in holy Communion is one of the most attractive features of become a Christian?

Yes, a Christian and a Catholic. Intercommunion with other denominations is not permissible. There has to be agreement on the true nature and character of the Blessed Sacrament. Catholics are called up to receive Christ in the Eucharist often and worthily. They are to walk in harmony with Christ and in his good graces.

Then explaining Christ's true presence in the Eucharist must be primary and paramount for the evangelizer. Shouldn't men and women be eager to share this great blessing with those interested in the faith?

Yes, they should. Jesus is love itself. He is God made man, the second Person of the Trinity. There is no greater attraction to a person than a person's love. The Church has a pastoral instruction relating to its document on social communication promulgated at the Second Vatican Council, saying: "Communication is more than an expression of ideas and the indication of emotion. At its most profound level, it is the giving of self in love. Christ's communication was, in fact, spirit and life. In the institution of the Eucharist, Christ gave us the most perfect form of communication between God and man possible in this life" (§11).

Just about every answer to my questions refers to Jesus Christ. It is clear that those who evangelize must have their lives centered on him. Is that so?

Yes. Pope Paul VI, who wrote the modern document on evangelization, *Evangelii Nuntiandi (On Evangelization in the Modern World)*, said this in a homily: "Not to preach the gospel would be my undoing, for Christ himself sent me as his apostle and witness. The more remote, the more difficult the assignment, the more my love of God spurs me on. I am bound to proclaim that Jesus is Christ, the Son of the living God. Because of him we come to know the God we cannot see. He is the firstborn of all creation; in him all things find

their being. Man's teacher and redeemer, he was born for us, died for us, and for us he rose from the dead."

Pope Paul VI was surely convincing, wasn't he?

He was inspired and single-minded. In another one of his homilies he said: "Remember: it is Jesus Christ I preach day in and day out. His name I would see echo and reecho for all time even to the ends of the earth."

Through the Catholic teaching on the Eucharist, Christ, in effect has never left us. He continues to be present and accessible. Jesus Christ, present in the tabernacle, is the heart and center of our parishes. How privileged are those who have access to Christ, who spend quiet moments before the Blessed Sacrament.

This is certainly a beautiful teaching for those who have faith.

It is. Jesus said, "Come, follow me." The invitation is there. Evangelizers do well to make use of every opportunity to proclaim Christ. As the hymn says: "You satisfy the hungry heart with gifts of finest wheat."

Something Extra

What do Catholics believe about the Eucharist?

At Mass, Catholics believe that the body and blood of Jesus is really present, not just symbolically, in the Eucharist under the appearances of bread and wine. At Mass, we receive Jesus' real body and blood.

In the gospels, Jesus instituted this holy sacrifice. In Matthew, Jesus "took a loaf of bread, and after blessing it he broke it, and gave it to the disciples, and said, 'Take, eat; this is my body.' Then he took a cup, and after giving thanks, he gave it to them, saying, 'Drink from it, all of you; for this is my blood'" (Mt 26:26–28). In John, he said: "I am the living bread that came down from heaven. Whoever eats of this bread will live forever; and the bread that I will give for the life of the world is my flesh" (Jn 6:51). John continues: "The Jews then disputed among themselves, saying, 'How can this man give us his flesh to eat?' So Jesus said to them, 'Very truly, I tell you, unless you eat the flesh of the Son of Man and drink his blood, you have no life in you'" (Jn 6:52–54).

Saint Paul also affirms the Real Presence. He says: "The cup of blessing that we bless, is it not a sharing in the blood of Christ? The bread that we break, is it not a sharing in the body of Christ?" (1 Cor 10:16).

CHAPTER TWELVE

Intimidation

Why aren't there more Christians reaching out to enlighten those without a relationship with God? Shouldn't there be more people inviting the unchurched to become members in their faith community?

There should be more reaching out. Those who value their relationship with God through Christ should extend the hand of friendship. Perhaps they consider their relationship with God a personal thing, that they have no responsibility to the faith life of others. We are creatures of habit. When habit becomes commonplace, the common way of living, men and women are enculturated. Christianity is not meant to be that way. This is not what Jesus wants. He sends his followers to the ends of the earth to proclaim the "Good News" of God's love.

So there is fear?

Intimidation! The word, comes from the Latin word, *timor*, which means "fear." Yes, there is fear. Jesus sent his apostles out on a mission. Saint Matthew's Gospel relates how they were to visit towns and villages proclaiming the kingdom of God and calling people to repentance. Jesus anticipated their fear.

What did he say?

He said the harvest was great but the laborers were few. Serious challenge awaited them. He said, "Have no fear of men!" Jesus told them that everything that was hidden would be revealed. They should not fear those who can kill the body, but those who can do away with both body and soul. "Everyone therefore who acknowledges me before others, I also will acknowledge before my

Father in heaven; but whoever denies me before others, I also will deny before my Father in heaven" (Mt 10:32-33).

Strong words! He knew their mission was not an easy one.

Christ told them that anyone who did not love him more than father or mother or son or daughter was not worthy of him. Jesus was not doing away with the Fourth Commandment, "Honor, your father and your mother," but his followers had to understand that they were doing God's work.

It is clear that Christ was not into compromise. He was to come first, qualifications and conditions notwithstanding. Is my sense of this on the mark?

Yes. This is a matter of maturity. Children learn love and experience love from their parents. Christ does not suggest that they should love their mothers and fathers less. But as children grow, advance in wisdom and knowledge, they come to know that God is the source of everything. God gave them their parents. God is the giver of all their blessings. Nothing has priority over God. The disciples of Jesus were about

to venture forth in a very hostile world, an unforgiving world, a world that would threaten them with martyrdom.

We are merely flesh and bones. Is it possible to succeed as human beings under such a tremendous burden?

The grace of God was with his apostles. They were inspired and motivated by the Holy Spirit. Christ knew all this. He predicted that his first pope, Saint Peter, would deny him. Intimidated in the courtyard of the high priest Caiphas, Peter told a maidservant that he knew nothing about Jesus. And a cock crowed! Christ declared, "Before the cock crows, you will deny me three times, Peter."

But Peter proved himself in time, didn't he? Isn't he revered as a saint?

Yes. After Jesus' Resurrection, along the Sea of Galilee, Christ asked Peter, his first pope, "Do you love me?" Peter affirmed his love. Twice more Christ asked, "Do you love me?" And Peter, remorseful and repentant, said, "You know that I love you." Then Jesus said, "Feed my lambs! Feed my sheep." He entrusted the care of the flock into Peter's hands. Saint Augustine makes this observation about Saint Peter: "The triple confession of your love is to regain what was lost three times by your fear. You must loose three times what you bound three times; untie by love that which your fear bound. Once, and again, and a third time did the Lord entrust his sheep to Peter."

I am beginning to think this business of evangelization is too much for the ordinary Christian.

Not really! If a Christian is interested in the eternal salvation of friends and neighbors, he can simply encourage them. Catholics can invite people to the already existing parish programs of instruction. They can offer to accompany newcomers to worship at Mass. There are any number of things that can be done. Evangelizers are not required to have academic degrees. The apostles were fishermen. Remember that we do not live under the same hostile conditions of the early disciples. The Roman Empire no longer exists. It is true that in some countries evangelization is

prohibited. Christians are imprisoned and intimidated, but this is not the case here in the United States.

I should think that people are intimidated for other reasons. What if they fear being branded "extremists" or "Jesus freaks"?

That's possible. But if evangelizers are sincere in heart and level-headed, they know name-calling is simply part of the game. Jesus experienced name-calling, too. "For John came neither eating nor drinking, and they said, 'He has a demon'; the Son of Man came eating and drinking, and they say, 'Look, a glutton and a drunkard, a friend of tax collectors and sinners'" (Mt 11:18–19).

Evangelization is a dirty word to some people. They identify the effort with high-pressure home visitors. Men and women knock at your doors and try to overpower you with quotations from Scripture.

Certain denominations do send representatives to neighborhood homes. They come with an agenda and a carefully thought-out approach that may be overwhelming to some. Their reputation for being overly aggressive is widespread. This is not true evangelization. While Jesus himself had a magnetic personality and the crowds flocked to him, his rapport was always respectful of people's freedom. He said, "Learn of me for I am meek and humble of heart." Those who evangelize improperly make the challenge even more difficult for true evangelizers. High-pressure selling creates a climate that is not conducive to receiving God's word.

If Jesus was so pleasing to the crowds, why was he hounded by the scribes and Pharisees and chief priests?

Jesus cured the sick. He blessed people with miraculous healings. They saw him as a man of compassion. The religious leaders of Christ's day saw his ministry otherwise, even as a threat to their own positions of honor and respect. They tried to cast doubt on Jesus as a man of God, to discredit him. Their hearts were not in the right place. Their dispositions proved to be stumbling blocks to faith in him. They were unwilling to change.

The conversion process is part of evangelization. It seems to me that potential Christians have to be willing to change their lives. Are evangelizers hesitant to outline this aspect?

"The Holy Spirit is the principal agent of evangelization" (*A Summary: On Evangelization in the Modern World*, §75). Evangelizers are not working alone. They pray for God's graces. With God, all things are possible. Jesus said, "Fear is useless. Trust is needed." The invitation to personal conversion will not fall on deaf ears. Jesus would not say "repent, and believe" if it were not possible. Evangelizers are men and women of faith. They have confidence in God and in their mission.

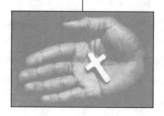

Something Extra

What is the Catholic Church anyway? Often I see the pope on TV during the evening news. The Church seems to be made up of a lot of pageantry and berobed bishops. Is that all there is?

T he first level of Church organization is the local parish, which is administered by a pastor with the assistance of other priests and religious, lay ministers (ushers, lectors, eucharistic ministers), and the advice of a parish council. The second level of Church is the diocese, which is a distinct geographical territory administered by a bishop, appointed by the pope and assisted by the council of priests and other coadjutor bishops. The third level of Church is the archdiocese, which is a cluster of dioceses in an area that are administered by an archbishop. The fourth level of Church is the national conferences of bishops composed of all the bishops in a particular country and presided over by an elected president who is one of the bishops. The fifth level of Church is the universal Church (it includes all Catholics in the Eastern and Western Church), which is ministered to by the pope with the assistance of the cardinals and the curia (committees that administer church policies). Despite the organizational complexities of the Catholic Church, it is more than just its officials, or buildings, or liturgy, and teachings—it is all of us united with Jesus Christ and related to one another through him, our Head.

CHAPTER THIRTEEN

Getting to Know You

It seems to me that the ordinary Catholic, the man, the woman in the pew, feels inadequate in sharing their faith about Jesus. Protestants appear to identify themselves with the Bible more than Catholics. Is this an accurate observation?

I don't know if there are any surveys on the matter. Protestants, the hundreds of denominations, are rather lumped together in your assessment. One of the original Protestant tenets is that the Bible is the sole rule of faith. It is certainly a good thing to read the sacred Scriptures. Catholics and Protestants have this in common. But the Bible is not the only and exclusive rule of faith. Jesus established a Church, a living authority, a living voice, to guide souls. Tradition, that is, the official way of relating to God, is also a rule of faith. The manner in which

the Church taught and worshiped in union with Christ from the beginning is valid Tradition. Everything Jesus said, and everything that Jesus did, is not contained in the Bible. "Now Jesus did many other signs in the presence of his disciples, which are not written in this book" (Jn 20:30).

What I mean is that Protestants seem to quote more readily from the Bible. Is it possible that they are more familiar with Jesus and his life?

Again, this is difficult to determine. Some Protestants may read their Bibles often, even daily. On the other hand, so do some Catholics. Despite the encouragement to read the Bible frequently, it is probably a safe statement to say that most Christians do not read the sacred Scriptures enough. Bibles gather dust on shelves. My guess is that there is no other book that has had more publication. Nevertheless the axiom remains true:"You can lead a horse to water, but you can't make him drink."

So there is no better way to make Jesus known than getting someone to read one of the gospels?

Yes. The reading of the Bible, especially the New Testament, is greatly encouraged. The "getting to know you" process goes on all the time. It happens between grandpas and grandmas and their grandchildren, between sweethearts, and neighbors, and fellow workers, and parishioners, and so on. The same is true about cultivating a personal relationship with Jesus Christ. There has to be an ongoing association, a sharing, an exchange of ideas.

This is a recommendation for evangelizers?

Yes! This is a good recommendation for evangelizers and for all Christians because, hopefully, all are potential evangelizers. This is not new. Saint Dominic (1170–1221), a great preacher in medi-

eval times, used to carry the Gospel of Matthew and the Letters of Saint Paul with him all the time. He knew them almost by heart. This saintly founder of the Dominican Order encouraged his priests and brothers to read the Old and the New Testaments faithfully.

There is always a presumption that those reading the Scriptures will communicate God's word. They are not meant to be merely bookworms. How do you motivate them?

Saint Dominic prayed that God would instill a genuine love in his heart for the salvation of all people. He believed that only then would he be a true member of Christ, who offered himself totally for every person. Dominic had love in his heart. He knew Jesus well. Christ's influence extended itself. You have to have it in order to give it. A daily reading of the New Testament, especially the gospels, transports the reader to Jesus' world. Reading the Bible is a time-honored and spiritually profitable practice. The process of getting to know you leads to getting to like you. And it is not just a matter of liking when it comes to Jesus. There is a transforming motivation that inspires a person to reach out and to love others.

Jesus is not like other historical figures. Is that so?

Jesus is not merely a historical figure. If this were so, we would erect a statue of him in the park like so many other prominent figures of the past. We may admire the Washingtons and Grants and Lincolns. Jesus, on the other hand, is loved, because he is God, a divine Person, who became one of us, a human being, without losing his divinity. He reestablished the loving relationship with the heavenly Father, which was lost by our sins. We look at the crucifix and cherish it, because it is the ultimate symbol of God's love.

I don't suppose it is possible to be an evangelizer without knowing something about Jesus. He himself is God's good news.

We sing the praises of movie stars, television personalities, sport figures, and recording artists. There does not seem to be any difficulty in relating the details of their lives. Magazines

make a living on this very thing. Money and fame are the prime movers. Jesus is in a category all by himself. Eternity hinges on faith in him.

How does the gospel describe the life of Christ?

All the books in the Bible are inspired. God inspired the individual writers.

While they retained their own personalities and writing styles, the content of the sacred Scriptures is guided by God. The four gospels were penned by eyewitnesses—Matthew and John, and companions of the apostles, Luke and Mark. These writers set down the pertinent details about Christ that will last until the end of time. Their value is timeless and applicable in every age. Every reader, with the grace of God, finds, in the life and love of Christ, whatever is needed to relate to God. Of course, the Church's guidance and interpretation clarifies the true meaning of the accounts.

It almost seems unbelievable that these short volumes are capable of such great impact.

The New Testament relates to Jesus. His love is communicated in his teachings. These are simple, but sublime. There is no "eye for an eye" or "tooth for a tooth" direction for life. Rather, we must love our enemies, and do good to those who persecute us. Jesus tells stories and parables. These are about the kingdom of God, how it develops, what it is like. Those who are familiar with Christianity, who know the Catholic faith, realize it is the religion of Christ. His teachings and the teachings of the his Church are one.

Of course all Christians do not practice what they preach. The teachings of Christ are not caught up in the lives of his followers, are they?

Honest Christians will tell you that they fall short of the ideal. Nevertheless, the love of Christ is caught up in the lives of those who practice their faith. Good example is impressive. A widower who recently lost his wife tells of a great consolation in his time of grief. One of the couple's friends told him that she was under instructions to become a Catholic. He and his wife, faithful to Sunday worship and the Christian life, had inspired their friend. No one should underestimate the grace of God and the embodiment of Christ's love in the lives of Christians.

Reading the gospels helps us to know Jesus. Do you expect the sheer weight of the words and the compelling story to instill love in our hearts for Jesus?

"God's love was revealed among us in this way: God sent his only Son into the world so that we might live through him. In this is love, not that we loved God but that he loved us and sent his Son to be the atoning sacrifice for our sins. Beloved, since God loved us so much, we also ought to love one another. No one has ever seen God; if we love one another, God lives in us, and his love is perfected in us" (1 Jn 4:9–12). This is very meaningful and significant quotation. Saint John puts it succinctly. It is our prayer that everyone who comes to know Jesus Christ will love him. Everyone who loves Jesus hopefully will be eager to share their love and faith with others.

Something Extra

What do you really mean by the word evangelization?

T wenty-five years ago most Catholics were not familiar with this word. Even today, if you quiz Catholics on their understanding of the word *evangelization*, some will respond with these associations:

- TV preachers asking for gifts
- Tent-revival meetings
- Young Mormons dressed in black canvassing from door to door
- Street-corner preaching

But these images do not represent the meaning of Catholic evangelization. Pope Paul VI in *On Evangelization in the Modern World*, says that evangelization is the process of becoming a disciple. He describes evangelization as a "…complex process made up of varied elements: the renewal of humanity (coming to know Christ), witness (living the life of a disciple), explicit proclamation (sharing Christ with others), inner adherence (the person chooses to follow Christ), entry into the community (sharing the Christian life with other disciples), acceptance of signs (the sacraments and sacramentals of the Church), and apostolic initiative (the person, now evangelized, now goes on to evangelize others)."

When the U.S. bishops issued their National Plan and Strategy for Catholic Evangelization, they said:

Evangelizing means bringing the Good News of Jesus into every human situation and seeking to convert individuals and society by the divine power of the Gospel itself. Its essence is the proclamation of salvation in Jesus and the response of a person in faith.

How can you recognize an evangelizing Catholic?

Susan Blum, who has written an evangelization training guide entitled *Share Your Faith* (Jeremiah Press, 1990), lists fifteen behaviors that should be encouraged among all Catholics.

1. Establish a friendly relationship with someone you don't know well.
2. Visit, in some setting, a stranger.
3. Share what it means to be a Catholic with others.
4. Speak with high regard of the Catholic Church, the parish, or the parish staff.
5. Encourage another to turn to God.
6. Share one's faith in God with another.
7. Tell a story about God's presence in one's life.
8. Assure another of how much God loves him or her.
9. Assure another of God's power.
10. Share with another what a difference Jesus makes in one's life.
11. Pray with someone privately or in a small group.
12. Pray with another, asking that person to let Jesus come into his or her life.
13. Invite someone to attend Mass.
14. Invite someone to go to a parish meeting.
15. Encourage someone to be of service to another.

CHAPTER FOURTEEN

Parents Are Evangelizers

Isn't it logical that children will get to know Jesus principally at home?

Yes! This is logical, providing mothers and fathers are Christian and sincerely following Christ. Parents do promise to lead their sons and daughters to Christ. When they come to Church to have their children baptized, they give these assurances. At the beginning of the baptismal ceremony the priest asks, "Do you clearly understand what you are doing?" They reply, "We do." This initiates a lifelong process. Mothers and fathers agree to pass the torch of faith to their sons and daughters. They are to make maximum effort to cultivate a love for Jesus Christ in the hearts of their children. It is a challenging, but a loving, quest.

How do parents go about this long-term effort of acquainting their children with the message of Jesus?

They do this by attempting to share the love they have for Jesus with their children. They do this by living a Christian life. They pray together. Family prayer fosters dialogue with God. Parents encourage their boys and girls to talk to Jesus personally and privately, too. Both memorized prayers and spontaneous conversation with God are encouraged. Do not underestimate the value of memorized prayers. The Lord's Prayer, the Our Father, comes directly from the lips of Jesus. This perfect prayer not only provides the wording, which is proper, but the phrasing itself defines how we should relate to the Father.

How early in their lives should parents pray with their children?

Immediately, even before birth! Children in the womb know their mother's voice, and become familiar with other sounds, too. Mothers are known to read to their unborn children. They pray for God's blessings for the new baby.

This seems to be very early. Do you think the children have any comprehension?

God knows the children even as they are being formed in the womb. Parents assist God in the formation of their offspring's character and spiritual well being. The tiny tots give glory to God in their infancy. There is an interesting line in Matthew's Gospel. Jesus says, "I thank you, Father, Lord of heaven and earth, because you have hidden these things from the wise and the intelligent and have revealed them to infants" (Mt 11:25). When children speak to God prompted by their mothers and fathers, this is like music to God's ears. Prayer is not just to reassure ourselves, but to give God glory.

Memorized prayers are more challenging to little boys and little girls. They hardly know what the words mean. Is this effort worth the time?

Comprehension takes time. This is true for all of us. We become familiar with sounds and words even before we learn our ABC's. Once upon a time there was a little girl named Julie, three years old. Julie had a brother named Herbert, who was five. Both the children knew the Apostles' Creed, the Our Father, the Hail Mary, and the Glory to the Father prayers by heart. No one taught them. They were members of a large household with several grownup aunts and uncles. The family prayed the rosary every evening after supper. If guests arrived they were invited to pray the rosary, too.

What else might parents do in their evangelizing efforts?

Celebrate the liturgical seasons. The family is sometimes called a little church. Children delight in events and happenings. A Catholic calendar highlights the same feasts celebrated in parish churches throughout the world. Customs and traditions enrich the lives of family members. They assist in forming a Christian mentality and a Catholic spirit. The life of Christ comes to life right in the home.

How about some examples?

The Advent wreath! This sacramental made of greens and four candles becomes the centerpiece of the dining-room table. Each day a prayer anticipating the coming of Christ at Christmas is read. The first candle is lighted during the first week of Advent. The children come to understand how the world waited for centuries for the coming of the Messiah.

And then the family sets up a Nativity set, a replica of the stable at Bethlehem?

Yes, and there are variations in observing this tradition. Some families may take the stable down from the attic at the start of the Advent season. The children assist in placing a little straw in the stable every day, reminded that the straw represents good deeds in anticipation of Christ. A figurine might be added per day, like a lamb, or a donkey. Parents explain how the Son of God had no place to be born. "He came unto his own and his own received him not."

What other church calendar events are featured in the home practice?

Lent! Pentecost! Feasts of Jesus, Mary, and the saints! Parents may wish to celebrate the saints days after whom their children are named in baptism. The boys and girls come to appreciate the lives and the patronage of their own saints. Perhaps they have a cake as they might on their birthday. Maybe they receive a gift, like a book telling about their very own saint. The saints become real people. The children learn that their saints loved God and served him perfectly.

What else could parents do as evangelizers?

They do well to have godly conversations with their sons and daughters. They ought to be certain that the children understand what life is all about. The children came from God and are to return to God. This is a matter of origin and destiny. Life is a journey. All life spans are limited. True perspective demands that people do not entertain the false notion that they are to live forever on earth. Destiny, life forever with God, is attained through Christ. Good is rewarded. Evil is punished. These are basic concepts. In this secular society there is no need to reinvent goodness or virtue by some other "socially acceptable" formula. Jesus is the way, the truth, and the life.

Would they read the Bible together?

Mothers and fathers buy children's books to encourage them to read. Among the books, the Bible should have a special place, especially Bibles designed for children. If they read or hear the passages selected for the coming Sunday readings at Mass, and discuss what Jesus said or did, this can foster greater understanding and appreciation. This way, youngsters can develop their religious knowledge and be inspired. The entire process contributes in the formation of the children's characters in the image of Jesus.

This would seem to be quite a learning experience for the parents, wouldn't it?

Everyone can learn by teaching. Unwittingly parents hone their skills in evangelizing adults while they are teaching their own children.

Mothers and fathers realize a sense of accomplishment when they assist others in their journey of faith. Is there truly any greater calling?

No. Parents prepare their offspring for reality. They sponsor them through schools and universities. They attempt to equip them for independent living and the challenges ahead. Sharing their faith in Jesus Christ is probably their most important contribution. Then it is hoped that their sons and daughters will share their own faith in Christ with their own families. They pass on the message of true, divine intervention, that the heavenly Father sent his Son Jesus to be their Savior, their Redeemer, and their friend.

Something Extra

Why do Catholics bother attending Church so often?
What's the attraction?

When you worship, your life is lined up properly. You see things in a better perspective. Attending Mass is an advantage—not an unnecessary or irrelevant act. Let nothing prevent you from attending Mass, no work schedule, classes, vacation, lack of transportation—nothing except genuine sickness or some truly valid reason.

Worship is not optional, for both the First and the Third Commandments set down the responsibility for keeping holy the Lord's Day. When we attend Mass, Jesus changes bread and wine into his Body and Blood. This is his Holy Sacrifice. Your mind and heart are opened to the readings during the Mass. They are the Word of God by which your soul is nourished. Remember, too, that Christ is truly present under the forms of bread and wine, so your soul is nourished when you receive holy Communion, for you are receiving Jesus Christ. After all, Jesus declares: "Unless you eat the flesh of the Son of Man and drink his blood, you have no life in you" (Jn 6:53).

CHAPTER FIFTEEN

Jesus Made House Calls

So your theory is that if parents are faithful in sharing God's plan for salvation through Christ with their children, they will become more comfortable talking to adults. Still, not all adults are receptive. Some may think that their religion is a personal matter and no one else's business. How does an evangelizer begin a conversation with an adult?

Well, a conversation about Jesus and his message should never be forced. Even though Christians should be interested in the salvation of all people (this is the mind of Christ), they must take their cues from Christ himself. Christ reached out; he did not stay in his hometown of Nazareth and say, "You folks can come to me." He went down from Jerusalem to Jericho. He traveled from Cana in Galilee to Samaria, even to the pagan territory of Decapolis. He visited the homes of Martha, Mary, and Lazarus, Simon, Matthew, Zacchaeus, and more.

Then Christianity seems to be a religion of reaching out, is it not?

Yes, it is not possible to understand the story of Jesus without entertaining the basic truth that God communicates. All the books in the Bible are accounts of the heavenly Father dealing with the men and women he created. Travelers and pilgrims who journey to Rome frequently visit the Vatican's Sistine Chapel. They look up to admire Michelangelo's masterpiece on the ceiling. The painting depicts God reaching from heaven and touching the outstretched hand of Adam. The sending of his Son is God's greatest communication. In Christ's earthly life he demonstrated that there is no substitute for personal contact.

What about door-to-door visitation?

This is one way to reach out. It has to be done respectfully. Some aggressive folks have left distasteful impressions. But it is an excellent practice. It is practical, because parishes often do not have the enormous sums of money needed for advertising. It is a noble effort because those visiting go in the name of Christ and in the spirit of Christ. It is a local effort. Parishes reach out to families in their areas.

After all, people do canvas neighborhoods for various causes. Children come calling to sell candy bars to support class trips, and the parish visitation or census has nothing to do with fund-raising, or running for public office, for that matter. The goals are higher and the motivation, too.

There are many occasions when people knock on doors. Politicians ring bells and press the flesh, if they want to be elected. Professional fund-raisers know that the cardinal rule of personal contact gets results; and, of course, it is a traditional, time-honored practice for priests to visit their parish families. Jesus himself set this good example. When there are so many more parishioners than priests, when the harvest is so great and the laborers are so few, the faith community is blessed to have parishioners active in visiting and in participating in all the aspects of the parish visitation effort.

So there should be visitation of all the families in the parish. Is that what you're recommending?

Ideally, they should call at every home in the neighborhood. That will mean a great number of contacts. Catholics are like parishioners of other faith congregations. Some practice their faith. Others are occasional worshipers. And there will be opportunities to speak to men and women who belong to no religion. There are millions of people who come from families that are indifferent to religion. Church-going was never in their experience and there is a good chance that even active Catholic families will not be acquainted with one another.

What do the visitors say when the doors are opened?

Usually they introduce themselves and explain that they are visiting on behalf of the local Catholic parish. Their purpose is to assist the pastor in updating the parish lists. There will be census cards to be filled out. These ask about names, addresses, phone numbers, the sacraments received, and the children's attendance at religious-education classes. Often there is a family member who is not Catholic, perhaps a husband or a wife. The visitors should not neglect to inquire if the non-Catholic is active in any faith community. They should ask if there is any interest in the Catholic faith. Not to show interest is, in effect, not to be interested. This is not Christ's way. It is possible that the non-Catholic has some interest. This is an occasion to encourage him or her.

Suppose they encounter anti-Catholic sentiment, even specific complaints? What should they do?

Listen with patience. If a person has suffered some injury or offense, be sympathetic. Tell them you will pray for them. If the complaint has merit, offer to communicate the information to the pastor. If there are technical or historical or scriptural questions, or even objections, let them know that the parish has ongoing religious instructions. Perhaps they may be interested in the RCIA (Rite of Christian Initiation for Adults) program. Never engage in argumentation. That is not the task of the home visitor. Parish priests are trained in theology and philosophy. If those visited are truly interested in finding answers, put them in touch. Ordinarily, the experience of parish visitors is positive. They are received cordially.

What do parishioners hope to accomplish with the parish census or visitation? Are the positive results evident?

The *Catechism of the Catholic Church* cites visiting the sick and the imprisoned as works of mercy. Parishioners may discover the aged and the infirm. Visiting all God's children in the town and neighborhood is a loving ministry. "But anyone united to the Lord becomes one spirit with him" (1 Cor 6:17). Visitors are simply showing interest in others.

They inquire if they may assist materially or spiritually. They provide information about Mass schedules, classes for baptism, religious-education classes, parish organizations and activities. They may explain about the parish council, the choir, devotions, outings, parish picnics, and pilgrimages. If a family has been out of touch, they are encouraged to return. The human heart longs for God, even if the mind does not always acknowledge it. Visitors may remind people that Christ is present in the tabernacle, always waiting for them during their times of stress or sadness. Providing information and encouragement has good results.

So this is all part of evangelization? Will the home visitors be talking about Jesus Christ?

The visitors may wish to share their faith in Christ if there is an opportunity. Interest is sometimes manifested in strange ways. Why do Catholics go to confession? Is it necessary to be baptized? Questions are often clues to what a person is searching for. The visitors are not to preach or proselytize, but they do well to

recognize that those being visited might not go to a Catholic rectory just to ask questions. However, they need to know that the parish priest is a friendly person, ready and willing to assist them in their journey of faith.

In a way I suppose they are taking Christ's place, aren't they?

The baptized are members of Christ's Church, referred to in the Bible as Christ's body. Jesus is the head. Parishioners are members of Christ's body. They are to walk his ways, do his deeds and speak his words. Jesus said, "I came that they may have life…" (Jn 10:10).

Is it appropriate for evangelizers and home visitors to invite those they meet to pray with them?

Yes. This may be accomplished by having the visitors distribute small cards with prayers on them. The prayer of Saint Francis, "Lord, make me an instrument of your peace," is a favorite. Mary's *Magnificat* prayer is also appropriate: "My soul proclaims the greatness of the Lord, my spirit rejoices in God my Savior" is how it begins. Spontaneous prayer is fitting also.

Something Extra

What are the hows of home visits?

The easiest and least expensive form of reaching out to others is the home visit. Even though many Catholics shy away from home visiting, other Catholics have always visited homes for a variety of reasons. In certain dioceses, it is traditional that every Catholic home be visited once a year. In other parishes, a census has been taken which often has involved visiting every household within the parish boundaries. And the Legion of Mary has done a version of house visiting ever since its inception in the early part of this century. Here are tips on making home visitation easier than most people imagine. This abbreviated list follows the advice laid out by Frank DeSiano, C.S.P., in *The Evangelizing Catholic: A Practical Handbook for Reaching Out* (Paulist, 1998).

1. Set up a plan to make home visitation a "doable" effort. Not every house in the parish need be visited. Pick a particular group of people (seniors, for example) or a targeted neighborhood, or people who have just moved into new apartment complexes or new housing developments. That way, the visiting effort can be limited and thus has an end point.

2. Design the visit with a particular purpose in mind. Not every visit should be an invitation for people to return to the sacraments or a request to accept the Gospel. People can be visited so that they can be told about various parish ministries, consulted about a particular parish effort (a Habitat for Humanity house or a day-care center), welcomed to the neighborhood, feel invited into the parish family, or surveyed about their needs and expectations. Even on these kinds of visits, be sure to have people visit in teams of two, most especially if one of the visiting team is a novice to this effort.

3. Since every set of visits is different, preparation for each type is unique. It would be good to role-play various encounters with lots of people giving feedback. It is essential to outline the message that visitors will bring, anticipate any materials that may be needed, and prepare for any eventuality.

4. Often it is very helpful to "script" a parish visit, just as market researchers follow a certain pattern in interviewing people. Some elements of a script might be as follows:

- A greeting, along with information about who you are and why you are there.
- Be upbeat and enthusiastic. The first minute in any encounter is most crucial.
- Ask permission to present a simple brochure about the parish to the householders.
- Ask if the household has any Catholics or people looking for a church.
- Invite Catholics to a particular meeting, event, or to visit the rectory.
- Ask if there are any questions that you can answer.
- Before you leave, ask if you can pray for or with any members of the household.
- Leave behind a neighborhood directory with names and addresses of local agencies as a "thank you" for their time.
- Make sure that people who go on home visits know that being spontaneous and natural is far more important than being highly trained.
- Make sure that visitors have a realistic attitude toward any outcomes. In a typical effort, only half the people will be at home. Of those that answer, most will respond with pleasantries but will quickly usher any visitors away; and of those that answer the door, probably only one in seven will actually engage in a meaningful conversation.

CHAPTER SIXTEEN

Building the Faith Community

When many people think of the Catholic Church, they think of the pope and his centralized authority in Rome. How do you explain his function?

The Holy Father, the pope, does reside in and administrate over a hundred acres within the city of Rome. His authority comes directly from Jesus. He has all three powers: judicial, legislative, and executive. Christ vested his authority in Saint Peter, the first pope. Each pope thereafter is a successor to Saint Peter. In his divine wisdom, the Lord knew this would be the best working system from age to age and including people of every race. But the Holy Father is not the Church all by himself. The Church encompasses the Catholic population worldwide, approximately a billion in a world population of close to six billion.

You are saying that Jesus did not just start a movement. He actually established a Church. How did this happen?

Generally speaking, an establishment, a moral body, is made up of people who are constituted and have authority. Jesus gathered disciples and apostles. He formed them by his teachings, he set down the specifics with regard to our relationship with God. He definitely bestowed authority. All three basic elements for a Church are clearly present. Men and women and children who believed in Jesus Christ became the Christian community.

How does this flow from Scripture?

Jesus said to Peter, "I tell you, you are Peter, and on this rock I will build my church, and the gates of Hades will not prevail against it. I will give you the keys of the kingdom of heaven, and whatever you bind on earth will be bound in heaven, and whatever you loose on earth will be loosed in heaven" (Mt 16:18-19). Keys are a sign of the authority that Christ granted to Peter and his successors. The correct interpretation of this passage has been clear from the very beginning.

So those who rallied around Saint Peter and the other apostles formed a faith community?

Yes. Saint Luke tells us, "The church throughout Judea, Galilee, and Samaria had peace and was built up. Living in the fear of the Lord and in the comfort of the Holy Spirit, it increased in numbers" (Acts 9:31). Also, Barnabas, a companion of Saint Paul, went to Tarsus looking for Paul "and when he had found him, he brought him to Antioch. So it was that for an entire year they met with the church and taught a great many people, and it was in Antioch that the disciples were first called 'Christians'" (Acts 11:26).

So Catholics living in countries all over the world are one Church. They constitute one family of faith?

The Latin word for church, *ecclesia*, which is based on the Greek word for a "calling out," means a convocation or an assembly. God is calling together his people from the ends of the world. The Greek word *Kyriake*, from which the English word *church* is dervied, as well as the German word *kirche*, means that which "belongs to the Lord" (*Catechism of the Catholic Church* §751-752). So church means convocation. "It designates the assembly of those whom God's Word 'convokes,' that is, gathers together to form the People of God, and who themselves, nourished with the Body of Christ, become the Body of Christ" (*Catechism of the Catholic Church, §777*).

So millions have come to belong to Christ's Catholic family of faith?

Yes. The word *catholic* comes from the Greek word meaning "universal." Christ came to save all people of every nation and race. In A.D. 110, Saint Ignatius, Bishop of Antioch, declared,

"Where Jesus Christ is, there is the Catholic Church." Ignatius succeeded Saint Peter who established the Church in Antioch before going on to Rome.

And Christ's apostles, his disciples, went from country to country evangelizing?

Yes! Around the Mediterranean basin, to gatherings and synagogues, from village to village and town to town, they carried the message. Saint Paul's travels are well known: Asia Minor, Greece, Macedonia, Rome, and so on. The apostles and disciples told the story of Jesus, how God promised a Messiah, a Redeemer, and this was fulfilled in Christ.

Ancient history tells of ten major persecutions of the Christians under the Roman emperors. What do you know about these?

The faith of the early Christians was outstanding. The odds appeared insurmountable. The first three centuries of Christianity are known as the Age of the Martyrs. But the faith community continued to grow. Today millions are members of Christ's family of faith. They came to know Jesus

Christ and to love him. The process has always been the same: first to know him; then to love him. They learned of Jesus through preaching and teaching. They were invited to renounce their sins and to embrace Christ. Christ's followers communicated. They brought the wonderful news of God's love in sending his Son. This is how the family of faith grows.

The Church says: "Anyone who rereads the Gospel accounts of the origins of the Church sees that the Church is intimately linked to evangelization: • The Church is born of the evangelizing activity of Jesus and the twelve apostles. • The Church, in turn, is sent by Jesus. The whole Church receives the mission to evangelize, and the work of each individual member is important to the whole" (*A Summary: On Evangelization in the Modern World*, §15).

Are all the baptized supposed to share in the building of the Church?

The Church is a living body. Parishioners in local parishes are to roll out the welcome mat for all who wish to know the reason for Christian optimism and hope. They do well to echo Christ who said,"Come to me, all you that are weary and are carrying heavy burdens, and I will give you rest" (Mt 11:28). Ideally, Christ is embodied in their lives. They realize that they are privileged to share in his mission. To this very day, the Church is built up through the love and respect of its members for Christ.

There must be interesting stories of conversion. The gospels tell of Mary Magdelene and Zacchaeus and Matthew and others. Who are some others of note?

Those who arrive on the doorstep of Christ's Church have their own stories to tell. Perhaps the grace of faith was occasioned by years of good example on the part of a practicing Catholic husband or wife. Maybe it happened to a sincere person after soul searching and devout prayer. Happy parishes themselves say a lot. As families, they reflect faith and joy.

Saint Augustine was a man with an unsavory past, but this good saint-to-be searched a long time for personal consolation and significance in his life. He is renowned for saying,"Our souls are restless, O Lord, and they will not rest until they rest in thee"

It is said that many Christians take their faith for granted until there is a genuine crisis in their lives. Then, they turn to the Lord and find strength. Does this happen often?

Yes. Personal suffering often is a path to God. It brings us to our knees. Suffering is not a bad thing if it leads followers of Christ to find consolation in him and in his Church. When parishioners love one another, they speak an irresistible language. They speak the language of Christ for all—even the suffering—to hear.

I guess that means that Christianity should be considered as a way of life. Is that so?

Jesus says, "I am the way, the truth, and the life." Evangelization is simply showing the way to Christ. Everyone is encouraged to share the wonderful treasury of this faith. The doors of Christ's Church are always open.

Something Extra

Do Catholics need to be evangelized?

Yes! Evangelization is beneficial to Catholics who already practice the faith. As Pope Paul VI points out, "The Church seeks to deepen, consolidate, nourish and make ever more mature the faith of those who are already called faithful or believers in order that they may further advance in the Christian life" (*A Summary: On Evangelization in the Modern World*, §54).

What about nonpracticing Catholics? Yes, again! A particular focus of the evangelizing Catholic ought to be those who have been baptized but who live outside the Christian life. We already know that a large number of the baptized have not formally repudiated their baptism but do not live in accordance with it. They resist the idea of evangelization out of indifference or a hostility based on a belief that he or she is one of the family, but is "in the know" and no longer believes.

Christ wishes God's love to be proclaimed and reproclaimed to all Catholics—practicing and nonpracticing. This is the essential mission that Christ gives his Church—to invite everyone to experience the full impact of God's love in Jesus.

CHAPTER SEVENTEEN

Parish Evangelization Committees

Does the Church require parish evangelization committees?

Canon law says that a bishop may have pastoral councils in his diocese. Setting up these councils is left to his choice. He decides how beneficial these advisory boards might be. A pastoral council might be on the diocesan level or on the local parish level, or perhaps on both levels. If there are pastoral councils, it surely would be helpful and appropriate to have active evangelization committees.

These are not decision-making bodies, are they?

They are advisory, not decision-making. The bishop has authority in his diocese, which is a given territory. The bishop appoints his priests as pastors in parishes. Neither the bishop nor his priests are to give up, to relinquish, the responsibilities that come with their positions. The pastors sign the checks, administrate their parishes, and make final decisions—all, however, in the spirit of Christ, and mindful of Christ's words, who wishes them to act as shepherds of souls. Recall what Matthew wrote: "You know that the rulers of the Gentiles lord it over them, and their great ones are tyrants over them. It will not be so among you; but whoever wishes to be great among you must be your servant, and whoever wishes to be first among you must be your slave; just as the Son of Man came not to be served but to serve, and to give his life a ransom for many" (Mt 20:25–28).

This exercise of authority is probably not understood by everyone. And I guess that parishioners need to have some insight into their own cooperative role, shouldn't they?

Often, there can be growing pains when parish councils act. What is needed is an appreciation of the true nature of the Church and of Jesus Christ. Printed guidelines for parish councils articulating the manner in which members cooperate are helpful. Conflicts can arise, but the example of Jesus should prevail.

How is a parish council structured?

There may be variations from diocese to diocese, but basically, councils serve to coordinate parish life as it relates to Jesus Christ. Members may be elected by parishioners, or even appointed by the pastor, to serve on the council. When the council meets, and after initial prayer and perhaps a short inspirational reading, there are reports from committees: liturgical, stewardship, religious education, social action, and evangelization. Those who serve on the council come to the meetings not so much as to solve problems but to make reports, coordinate efforts, and plan for the future. This method of organization does call for a special understanding. The council is not like other organizations, civic, social, political, and so on. The spirit of Christ must guide all of its deliberations, and all their deliberations, in the final analysis, are advisory.

So is there any training for parish council members? Are there courses provided?

My guess is that, in many places, there is no special formation for these positions, although this is an excellent suggestion. Those who are presently active in parish work are usually the ones selected to serve. They may also be selected because of some special expertise. For example, religious-education teachers would seem to be logical choices for the religious-education committee, and people with musical gifts might be suited to the liturgy committee. The more familiar parishioners are with the teachings of Christ and his Church, the better prepared they will be to serve.

Tell me how an evangelization committee might operate.

It is hoped that members of the evangelization committee will have read some of the books and publications on evangelization. Pope Paul VI's *Evangelii Nuntiandi (On Evangelization in the Modern World)* makes a good starting point. There are many other books and videos that can be used as resources. (See the suggestions on pages 153-154.)

The pastor would do well to meet with committee members and outline the challenges he sees in the parish. Evangelizers always work in harmony with the shepherds of the flock.

So is their focus exclusively on Catholics?

Pope Paul VI has this answer: "In the course of twenty centuries, the faithful have been tempted to narrow down the field of their missionary activity. Do not imprison the proclamation of the Gospel by limiting it to one sector of the population, to one class of people or to a single type of civilization. The Lord said, 'To the whole world! To all creation! To the ends of the earth!'" (*A Summary: On Evangelization in the Modern World*, §50). Nevertheless, there has been a tendency for Catholics to focus on Catholic programs, and a variety of parish renewal efforts.

Isn't it a good idea to go after the "lost sheep"? Isn't it appropriate to encourage those who do not worship the Lord on the Lord's Day to attend Mass faithfully?

Concern for nonpracticing Catholics has always been prominent. Jesus loves them. Evangelizers should pray for them and reach out tactfully. Saint Augustine expressed concern for those who were indifferent or lax in these words: "We entreat you, brothers, as earnestly as we are able, to have charity, not only for one another, but also for those who are outside the Church. Of these some are still pagans, who have not yet made an act of faith in Christ. Others are separated, insofar as they are joined to us in professing faith in Christ, our head, but are yet divided from the unity of his body. My friends, we must grieve over these as over our brothers. Whether they like it or not, they are our brothers; they will only cease to be so when they no longer say Our Father."

So is it a good idea for the evangelization committee to determine goals and set up specific programs?

They should work closely with their pastor who will assist them in getting a handle on the situation. A pastor is a shepherd. Jesus, the Good Shepherd, said, "I know mine, and mine know me." Goals and programs are fine. More important is stimulating a genuine love for those that Jesus loves and cultivating a longing in the hearts of parishioners to share their faith in Christ with others. They must truly want to encourage everyone to unite with Christ at Sunday Mass. They must yearn to have God's grace touch the hearts of unbelievers. Then, having nourished a desire to evangelize, they discern how to go about meeting the challenges.

Do they conduct surveys and engage in statistical analysis?

They may. Statistical analysis for dioceses, county by county, is available. This renders a picture of those already enrolled in different denominations. It indicates how many might be unlisted, or "unchurched," that is, those whose presence in church is very infrequent. For all purposes, the unchurched are not having their values reinforced by participation in a faith community.

So there are existing data on the frequency of Catholic participation at Sunday Mass?

Yes—plus parish priests often say that one-third of their people worship regularly; another one-third are occasional; and the remaining one-third hardly come to church at all. There are surveys indicating that about 32 percent of Catholics are faithful in uniting with Christ at Sunday Mass. Other surveys may offer a lower percentage. There was a survey done in Rochester, New York, saying that more than 60 percent of Catholics do not believe in the true Presence of Christ in the Eucharist. This seems to correspond with a Newsweek/CBS poll conducted in 1994. The parish pastoral council members ought to be aware of the extent of the evangelization challenge. The observation of Saint Augustine in the fourth century rings true. He said that there are those who may have recited the Apostles' Creed, but may not have made a personal, significant profession of faith.

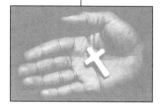

Something Extra

How would a plan for setting up a parish evangelization committee or team work?

Here is a set of recommendations based on the book *Creating the Evangelizing Parish* by Frank DeSiano, C.S.P., and Kenneth Boyack, C.S.P. (Paulist, 1993).

1. Designate a parish-evangelization coordinator. This should be someone enthusiastic about evangelization or someone already knowledgeable and interested in the issues of evangelization.

2. Select five to seven parishioners who will discern ways that the parish can evangelize more effectively. This group will have an overseeing role.

3. Prepare for action. This can include a day of prayer or retreat; study and understanding of Pope Paul VI's *On Evangelization in the Modern World*; Bible study; refresher course on the basics of the Catholic faith, and so on.

4. Enlist the cooperation of the pastor whose support, personnel decisions, and allocation of funds is central to the success of any evangelization effort.

5. Reach out to the broader parish population—to various parish committees and leaders—to seek support and advice on the evangelization effort.

6. With the pastor and the parish leaders, form a practical plan for evangelization. This plan should take into account the needs of the parish, such as evangelizing youth, fringe Catholics, Catholics who are no longer active, and reaching out to

people who are unchurched. The plan should include specifics, as well as a timetable for implementation, plus a period or method of evaluation.

7. Some sort of coming-together can initiate the participation of the whole parish in the evangelization effort. The efforts of everyone are necessary for success. The pastor can spearhead one communication effort by promoting the parish's commitment to evangelization in homilies, and in encouraging parishioners to extend a hospitable welcome to everyone in the liturgy, meetings, parish socials, and in all aspects of parish life.

8. Spread the evangelization theme to all members of the parish through announcements, homilies, mentions in the parish bulletin or newsletter, and encouragement of parish leaders. Parishioners need to see themselves as evangelizers in the larger secular community, among alienated Catholics, with coworkers, and with neighbors, friends, and family.

CHAPTER EIGHTEEN

Public Relations, Advertising, and Evangelization

How do parishioners, members of the evangelization committee, go about evangelizing? What are some proven methods?

Pope Paul's document, *Evangelii Nuntiandi*, cites these methods: witness, preaching, teaching, mass media, and person-to-person contact. Pope Paul emphasizes the following: "Evangelization exercises its full capacity when it achieves a permanent and unbroken intercommunication between the Word and Sacrament. The role of evangelization is to educate people in the faith in such a way as to lead each individual Christian to live the sacraments as true sacraments of faith" (*A Summary: On Evangelization in the Modern World*, §47). Popular piety is noted, too, insofar as it is rich in values, but it has its limits.

Parishioners are not commissioned to preach, but they may be of great assistance engaging in the many other approaches in faith-sharing.

So the role of parish evangelizers is one of a public relations effort?

In one sense, yes. Parish public relations ought to be the best. The love of Jesus Christ is to be reflected in all parish activities. The Church's public relations are not merely to create a good impression for the selling of products or services, and evangelization efforts are not simply to get people "on our team." Committee members can do much to foster a pleasant climate and to make known how Jesus Christ is embraced. Public relations is part of

evangelization but does not constitute its essence. Advertising is
helpful, too, as a means of making Christ known. Any advertising must be plausible, attractive,
and true.

*Give me an example or two of
the differences and distinctions
between public relations efforts
and evangelization.*

A pastor visits the Thursday
night bingo session in the parish
hall. He smiles and talks to the
players. He says he is evangelizing, but this may or may not be
accurate. Airline stewards also
smile and greet passengers. They
are not evangelizing. Their kindness and courtesy are greatly appreciated. The pastor's cheerful-
ness and good humor is appreciated, too. It is good to remember
that there is no evangelization if
you do not say "Jesus Christ." Of
course, all kindness and courtesy
is related to God's command to
love one another. It is unthink-
able that an evangelizer will neglect opportunities to prepare
the soil so the seeds of faith will
be well received.

*How would the evangelization
committee go about advertising?*

They should check out all the
free channels of communication
for particular events that the parish is sponsoring. If instruction
classes for adult converts are
about to begin, radio and television stations can air public service announcements. Newspapers usually will print announcements for nonprofit organizations
as a free service or at reduced
rates. Remember that the media
does need plenty of advance notice so that the announcements
can be scheduled.

What about paid advertising?

Radio and television stations
have rate cards, as do newspapers.
These rates should be researched
to get the most for the money.

*How might an ad be formu-
lated?*

Here is an example of some
possible printed ad copy: Would
you like to become a Catholic? Instruction classes are beginning at
St. Charles Parish on September
19. The teachings of Jesus Christ
and the Catholic Church will be
presented. Adults, Catholic and
non-Catholic, are encouraged to

attend. Parishioners welcome all men and women to their family of faith. Classes are presented free of charge. May we assist you in your journey of faith?

The advertisements should be simple and straightforward. They are invitational. Committee members should be patient and not expect extraordinary numbers. Those who are reached through the advertisements come to realize that the parishioners are interested in their spiritual welfare. The initial reaction may not be strong, but the communication process has begun.

Are committee members expected to develop the methods cited in the Paul VI's document on evangelization?

An excellent idea! With the exception of preaching, they can work to develop all the methods in their parish.

How might they develop "witnessing"?

To begin with, among themselves, they might write down an explanation of why they chose to be Christians. One priest has a sermon in which he asks the congregation, "Why are you Catho-lic?" Someone just might inquire. People understand that Catholics come from Catholic families. Their mothers and fathers and grandparents were Catholic. But the interest is centered on personal choice. The priest proceeds to give an answer from the pulpit. In conclusion, the homilist invites everyone to personalize their own stories, their own answers. Committee members might share their own stories among themselves in order to become accustomed to witnessing.

Is this common in Catholic circles?

Yes! Especially among those who have made Cursillos! A Cursillo is a type of retreat extending over three or four days. The word *cursillo*, from the Spanish, means a "short course in Christianity." It is a joyful event, a dynamic one. There is team approach in the presentations. Cursillos began in Spain more than forty years ago. They take place in many countries. There are thousands who have experienced this renewal of spirit. Those who have made Cursillos may wish to meet monthly in what are called Ultreyas. There is prayer and inspiration, and usually one of the Cursillistas gives a witness talk.

This experience must be very helpful in an evangelizer's "person to person" contact.

Yes. Christians, those who appreciate their faith in Jesus Christ, are eager to share with those who have no parish, no faith community, of their own. They are capable of telling others of the great consolation that they experience. Peer-to-peer sharing is meaningful, and it is effective, too. It is true that faith is a gift from God, but sincere Christians are instrumental in channeling God's grace. The confidence that Christians maintain during times of crisis is reflective of the faith they have in Christ. In times of sickness, when there is a death in the family, their faith sustains them. In their dealings with friends, neighbors, fellow workers, and peers, they bear witness to God and to Jesus Christ.

So is it a good idea to invite friends to other parish events?

Yes, indeed! To Sunday Mass! To first Communions and confirmations and weddings! To pot-luck suppers! To many other happenings! Make them feel welcome. Let them see how parishioners love one another.

How would the committee go about activating fellow parishioners to evangelize?

Workshops! Whatever it takes to cultivate a genuine interest in sharing their faith in Christ! Every baptized adult ought to be commissioned to share with others. All parishioners should pray that everyone will come to experience Jesus Christ. This is the essential mission of Christ's Church. One of the intentions to be cited frequently at Mass during the prayer of the faithful should be the gift of faith. Perhaps the sincere interest of the parish might be communicated in the weekly parish bulletin and in parish newsletters that are sent directly to homes. Invite speakers from the diocesan office for evangelization. Ask the pastor to talk about it from the pulpit. Does the parish have a welcome sign outside the church? Imagination and good will go a long way to making evangelization part of the fabric of a parish.

Something Extra

How should a parish roll out the welcome mat for new or returning Catholics?

B ecause Catholics form a eucharistic community of faith, welcoming and hospitality are hallmarks of a parish where evangelization is practiced. Here are some ways recommended by Frank P. DeSiano, C.S.P., in *The Evangelizing Catholic* (Paulist, 1998) to make sure people know they belong:

- Welcoming new parishioners
  — Attractive and easy-to-fill-out parish registration forms.
  — Direct welcome through a gathering where newcomers can meet one another as well as the pastor and representatives of the parish staff.
  — When people register, they need to be invited to participate in parish activities and need to have basic information about all aspects of parish life.

- Welcoming Sunday visitors
  — A greeting, especially to visitors and newcomers, should be given on Sunday by ushers or other parish volunteers.
  — Make sure that after-Sunday-Mass hospitality is true hospitality. Remind parishioners to introduce themselves to newcomers and to those they do not yet know.
  — Appoint some people at other church events (such as service projects or meetings) to make sure that everyone has been introduced to one another. Often people assume that all present already know one another.

— Set aside particular Sundays when parishioners are encouraged to bring visitors. On these occasions, be sure to have a Visitor's Sign-In Book and special welcoming material.

• Welcoming the whole neighborhood
   — Sponsoring festivals and celebrations to which the whole neighborhood is invited. The pre-Christmas season and the pre-Easter season are two such opportunities.
   — Parish commitment to certain neighborhood associations and activities.
   — Preparation of information brochures about the parish, created with the "non-Catholic" neighbor in mind.
   — Listing of the parish in the lobbies of nearby hotels, motels, campgrounds, and RV parks where tourists and business travelers might stay.
   — Sponsoring of concerts, musical programs, recitals, and plays whose appeal reaches out beyond the parish.
   — Undertaking responsibility for a certain community need, such as the food pantry or meals on wheels.

CHAPTER NINETEEN

Attitudes

Not every person accepted Jesus in his day, did they? Evangelizers, if they are realistic, must realize this same challenge exists today. What underlies such opposition to Christ?

There are attitudes and frames of mind that are not conducive to conversion. Jesus taught that unless we become like little children we will not enter the kingdom of God. He was not saying we must become childlike, naive, or gullible. He did say, "Learn of me for I am meek and humble of heart." Conversion must be based on a willingness to learn and to change.

Some people seem to resent religion as if they do not want to be told what to do. Does that ever happen?

I'll tell you a story in that regard. A priest was in a department store one day. A salesperson asked, "What parish are you with?" He explained that he was retired, but assisted in several parishes in the area. "And what parish are you with?" Father inquired. She replied, "I don't belong to any parish. I am an unbeliever." "You don't belong to any denomination?" he asked. She said, "I believe what I want to believe."

What does the evangelizer do in a case like that?

The priest told the salesperson, "God has communicated from the beginning of time. God communicated with our first parents, Adam and Eve." Father explained, "The first man and woman dared to disobey, to defy, God. God sent them away from paradise. Their original sin has affected people throughout history to this very day. But in his love, God promised to send a redeemer. The one he sent was his own Son, Jesus Christ. That was some two thousand years ago. Our calendar is based on the birth of Christ."

So the good father was evangelizing right on the spot, wasn't he?

Yes, even though there wasn't a great deal of time to converse, since another customer arrived. "God defines the relationship we have with him." The priest touched briefly on how relationships define our lives. Basketball players on the court follow the rules of the game. No goal tending, or traveling with the ball, or double-dribbling, or so on. In a department store the boss defines policy, the customer/employee relationship, courtesies, and so on. Husbands and wives, too, are guided by the parameters of a loving relationship.

Then what happened?

Nothing happened at that point. The priest took his package and left. The sale was over. The salesperson began to wait on another customer.

Her attitude seems to be common, a prevalent mind-set. People say they believe what they want to believe. Is it macho? Good old rugged individualism? Or is it just the American way?

It would almost seem that some people feel the freedom that they enjoy permits them to define their relationship with God. Notions of freedom are carried beyond the validity of an organized religion, beyond a Church. There is an impression that believers have freedom to the extent that they may choose how to relate and respond to God.

So "pick and choose" is included in the long list of challenges to evangelization. Is that true?

Yes. The labels "cafeteria Christians" or "cafeteria Catholics" have surfaced. If a family moves into a neighborhood, they look around to see which church suits them. This is understandable in one way. If, for example, there were several Catholic churches in the same city, some families might find the liturgical celebrations, the Sunday Masses, more lively, more interesting, more meaningful, at one church than another. But when it comes to celebrations that flow from Christ's teachings, it is a matter of integrity, of how one relates to God. If Catholics should decide that Sunday worship in another denomination was more attractive, even more fun, and they dismissed themselves from the Eucharist, this would be a serious breach of their faith.

Admittedly, there are Catholics who simply excuse themselves from Sunday worship. They do not bother to worship at all. What underlies their attitude and lack of participation?

If a Christian really believes that Jesus Christ is truly present at Mass offering himself to the heavenly Father, then, all the king's horses and all the king's men will not keep that Christian away. Faith is at the heart of adoration and worship.

Do the nonpracticing Christians offer any specific excuses? Is there any research on this?

At a workshop in one diocese entitled "Encouragement for Nonpracticing Catholics," the participants, who were themselves

practicing, observed the following underlying causes of Catholics falling away from the faith: the nonpracticing folks do not feel that they belong, boring celebrations, divorce, birth control, do not feel that they need to go to church to pray, unpleasant encounters with priests, married outside the Church and do not feel welcome, misunderstandings, feeling of alienation, changes since Vatican Council II, do not see its importance in their eyes, they have been hurt, laziness, missed Mass a few times and got into the bad habit, and so on.

Quite a list! Any suggested solutions?

Yes! The participants suggested the following: invite them to Mass, offer to accompany them, tell them they are missed, visit them, ask about their reasons for nonpractice, show them there is a need to worship, there is a need to thank God, that God needs them to carry on his work, that church is for sinners not the righteous, offer to pick them up, provide opportunities to experience the love of Christ in the Church, and so on.

For the most part these challenges do not seem insurmountable, especially with the grace of God.

Many of these challenges are public-relation matters. Companies and service-related enterprises know very well they have to extend kindness and courtesy in order to succeed in business. Saint Paul tells us, "If you do not have the spirit of Christ, you do not belong to Christ." Christians are to love God for God's sake and to reflect their love. Their love and concern must be at a higher level than any commercial effort.

So the problem really goes deeper?

Yes. We have to ask the question: Were the nonpracticing people in love with Jesus Christ in the first place? Was there an individual and personal relationship cultivated with Christ? Was there ever a point in the maturing process when they valued their faith in Christ and saw it as the only way of life? Only the individual can answer these questions. There may be many other factors.

What other factors?

It is possible that when they were growing up that their parent's faith was weak, that their mothers and fathers seldom participated in church. The habit of worship was not formed. Did their parents renege on the promises made at their children's baptism—the promises that they would assist their sons and daughters in developing a love and rapport with Christ? Maybe this obligation never dawned on them because their understanding of religion was so minimal.

So now what?

Evangelize! Introduce them again to Jesus Christ! Assist them to make the connection with Jesus' true presence in the Eucharist. Pray for them.

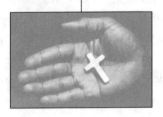

Something Extra

What kinds off things do inactive Catholics say when asked to consider returning to the Church?

"I've been gone so long I don't know what's going on in the Catholic Church anymore or how to act if I came back."

"I'm not interested. I have become an atheist. I no longer believe in God. Religion is just a crutch."

"Yes, Yes! I have just been waiting for someone to ask me."

"I think it's too complicated to be a Catholic. I wanted to get my son confirmed, and the priest insisted that he take some classes. My husband said: 'If they're going to make things that tough for us, let'em keep their Church.'"

"You must have been reading my mind. Ever since my baby was born I have been thinking about getting back to the Church."

"I'm a secular humanist and a member of the Ethical Society of America in spite of all my Catholic education. The Catholic Church just isn't relevant anymore."

"I wonder if God is behind this. I have been out of the Church for over thirty years, and lately I've been feeling something tugging at me. Maybe I better give the Church another chance and see what you have to say."

"No, I was a Catholic for twenty-four years and then got converted to the Church of God. Now I know how evil the Catholic Church really is. What do you think of that?"

"I'm impressed that someone would come out and look me up. I like that someone seems to care."

CHAPTER TWENTY

Divorce and Remarriage

Are there circumstances preclud-ing people from becoming Chris-tians and members of Christ's Church?

All who wish to follow Christ are welcome. They become his followers on his terms. They accept the challenge of taking up their crosses. They agree that his way of life and his relationship to the heavenly Father is the only path to follow.

Jesus warned his followers that it would be difficult. He even said that it could tear apart families. Christians living in the first three centuries during the Roman domination knew what torture, deprivation of civil rights, and martyrdom were all about.

But what about today?

Challenges still exist, but in different forms. Society is not menaced by governments to conform

in a religious manner. Society in the United States, and in some other countries, has become secular. God and religion have been eliminated from the common way of life. Culturally the religious dimension of life is greatly diminished.

How specifically?

In many ways! One prominent factor is the acceptance of divorce and remarriage.

The breakup of marriages is commonplace. This has great impact on children and family life. Are you saying a divorced person cannot become a Christian?

I am not saying that. There are many devout and dedicated Christians who are divorced. But there is a need for understanding. It is important to reconcile

Christ's words and the phenomenon of our times.

What did Jesus teach about divorce?

On one occasion the Pharisees asked Christ about divorce. He said: "But from the beginning of creation, 'God made them male and female. For this reason a man shall leave his father and mother and be joined to his wife, and the two shall become one flesh....' Therefore what God has joined together, let no one separate" (Mk 10:6-9). A little while later his disciples questioned Jesus about this same matter. He said to them: "Whoever divorces his wife and marries another commits adultery against her; and if she divorces her husband and marries another, she commits adultery" (Mk 10:11-12).

So those who divorce and remarry commit adultery. Is this true?

The sixth and ninth commandments of God are clear. Adultery is seriously sinful. Objectively speaking, whoever defies God by divorcing and remarrying lives in sin. But it is quite another matter to make judg-ments about particular unions. There are many couples who are divorced from their previous spouses and remarried. They may not be living in sin. Some explanation is called for here. This is not double talk, but explanation based on principle.

Go ahead! I am listening.

God instituted marriage. This is God's plan. This is God's way. God does not make mistakes. God actually joins the man and the woman in marriage. They are no longer two, but one. Jesus is clear. "What God has joined together, let no human separate." The authority to join people in marriage belongs to God. Catholics stand before the priest and two witnesses and before the altar. They solemnly vow to take each other as husband and wife. They make a contract. They promise to take each other as husband and as wife "for better, for worse, for richer, for poorer, in sickness and in health, until death do us part." That contract holds. God confirms and verifies the marriage contract. Christ's Church, adhering to his teaching, recognizes the validity and permanence of the marriage contract.

Everybody knows that there are thousands of Catholics who have been married and divorced and again remarried in the Church. They freely receive Christ in holy Communion, the Eucharist. How does this happen?

It is comforting to know that Christ loves everyone, including those unlucky in love. He reaches out in love to the married and to the divorced. The Church does, too. There is great sympathy and compassion. There is also firm adherence to principle. Many divorced people come to Christ's Church asking if their first marriage contract was valid. They request that Church officials look into the circumstances of their first marriage. They assist the Church by providing information and details. After some investigation, the Church is able to make a judgment. It is able to say if the marriage contract was or was not valid. If the marriage contract was null, then a declaration of nullity, or an annulment, is granted. This usually gives them a green light if they wish to remarry.

So is the annulment process long and involved?

It depends on the kind of case. Some are quite simple to determine. Others are called "formal" and take time because of complications. Parish priests assist petitioners in preparation for their submission to the diocesan marriage tribunal. Some dioceses have organized laypersons to assist in the preparation of cases as well.

Presumably those who marry do so in good faith. They intend to contract marriage validly. What would render a marriage contract invalid?

The Church has always recognized diriment impediments to marriage. Among those cited: force and fear, consanguinity, affinity, and so on. Within the past forty years, the Church has begun to recognize the invalidity of marriage on psychological grounds. Canon law 1095 reads: "They are incapable of contracting marriage: (1) who lack the sufficient use of reason; (2) who suffer from grave lack of discretion of judgment concerning essential matrimonial rights and duties which are mutually given and accepted; (3) who are not capable of assuming the essential obligations of matrimony due to cause of a psychic nature."

What does this boil down to?

The canon lawyers and experts in the diocesan marriage tribunal are versed in these cases. Thirty or forty years ago there were perhaps about three hundred to four hundred annulments granted in the United States. Today there are many more. Each submission to the tribunal is evaluated and substantiated. Regarding Canon 1095, it is safe to say that a great number are judged null because of the psychological grounds of immaturity. Those who work in marriage tribunals try to assist those whose lives have been disrupted, whose marriages have ended in tragedy. Their work is a work of compassion and mercy. It is also a work of justice. Their decisions must be based on truth.

Psychological grounds? Does this mean that one or both parties in marriage were not psychologically capable at the time of the contract? That they lacked

due discretion? That this goes to the essence of marriage?

In some way, one or both of the parties lacked what the Church regards as essential in making the life-long contract. In the United States today, about 50 percent of marriages end in divorce. This statistic is a commentary in itself. Marriage, according to God, is meant to be permanent, "until death do us part." If an individual, with little or no training in aviation, decided to take the controls of a plane and fly, he would be courting disaster. It is not good to judge particular cases that end in divorce, but it is safe to say that a great number people marrying today are not ready to fly.

Should evangelizers shy away from inviting divorced people from following Christ?

Absolutely not! Jesus came to save every person on earth. He loves each of us with a tremendous and never-failing love. Parishes abound with active parishioners who have lived through the challenge and tragedy of divorce and are remarried.

Something Extra

What are some things to do in reaching out and speaking about the Good News of Jesus Christ.

1. When speaking to a group of people, do not assume that every person in the audience is a Christian. Because we are a melting pot of many different paths and religious traditions, you may encounter a good many non-Christians in your evangelization efforts.

2. Make sure that your words and actions show a deep respect for each person's decision to believe in his or her own way. Our ecumenical society is based on this belief.

3. Use direct and straightforward language that transmits your message in a simple way. Don't try to use "fancy" words or clichés. Try to find fresh ways to get your message across.

4. Explain things as you go along. Don't assume that people understand what you are saying. Be prepared to give information on everything from what is a sacrament to what are the Gospels and where are they found.

5. Be a truth-teller. Do not shade the truth in order to make it more appealing. Be clear and accurate even if some listeners may find what you are saying distasteful.

CHAPTER TWENTY-ONE

Overcoming Obstacles

Is there anyone an evangelizer would not invite to participate in parish life? Non-Catholic divorced people may wonder if they would be welcomed? Would they be?

Welcome everyone! Those who are non-Catholic may attend Mass and join with parishioners in many activities. Communion, receiving Christ in holy Communion, is only permissible for Catholics who judge themselves worthy and in the state of God's good graces.

If a divorced non-Catholic became interested in becoming a Catholic, what is the procedure?

Make the person feel welcome and at home in the Catholic Church. Jesus loves them. They are encouraged to worship faithfully. Introduce those interested in taking instructions in the faith to the parish priest. He will be able to determine the challenges in each particular case. He wishes to assist the interested person in his or her journey of faith. He wishes to be straightforward and clear on what is required to follow Christ. Often he will have to explain Christ's teaching on the permanence of marriage. He will explain whether it is necessary or not to seek the Church's judgment in the validity of their marriage contract.

This could be complicated, especially if those interested were married and divorced more than once.

Patience and prayer is appropriate. If the man or woman is sincerely interested in becoming a Christian, a follower of Christ, the good Lord will assist with his grace. Those who work in marriage tribunals do have people who have experienced several marriages submitting their cases. Parish priests throughout the country try to help regardless of complications.

How about an example!

One pastor worked with a woman who was previously married three times. She was baptized in a Protestant church when she was young. Her first marriage was to another baptized non-Catholic. Her second marriage was to a Catholic, but not in the Catholic Church. Her third marriage was to a non-Catholic. The pastor assisted her in preparing a petition for an annulment in her first marriage. It took about a year to obtain. Her second husband died and this was confirmed by a death certificate. She filed a petition for an annulment in her third marriage.

Then what happened?

She received a declaration of nullity for her third marriage. During this time she attended Sunday Mass and also participated in other parish devotions, particularly adoration of the Blessed Sacrament. From the start she said she wished to become a Catholic. The pastor gave her books to read. On occasion she and other interested people visited with the priest, asking questions and listening. She was received into the Church. She and her new Catholic husband were married at the parish church.

Nice story! It has a happy ending. She managed to overcome many obstacles. What are some of the other obstacles that might stand in the way of becoming a Christian?

There are some other kinds of obstacles as well. Jesus does not call us to repentance without reason. Men and women have to learn about Christ and his Church before being baptized, before entering the Church. Over several months, candidates, sometimes called catechumens, pray, attend Mass, and gradually become integrated into the life of the parish. In the RCIA, the Rite of Christian Initiation of Adults, there are prayers said over them in ceremony. They work in harmony with God and accept his graces. If there is anything not compatible with Christ in their lifestyles, this has to be addressed.

This approach seems reasonable. Immigrants and foreigners who wish to become American citizens study the requirements. They learn about the United States. They accept the Constitution and, in loyalty, take a solemn oath. They become bona fide citizens.

Nice comparison. If there are matters that they entertain that are not in conformity with our country, they would not be permitted to become citizens. With the Church it is different inasmuch as they are pledging loyalty to God. If there was anything seriously incongruous with the will of God, there would not be a bona fide conversion to Christ.

Some examples would help.

A drug dealer would have to reform, give up his immoral and illegal profession, before entering Christ's Church. He may not continue to offend God if he decides to follow Christ. His life has to change. He has to make that decision, that choice. He has to cross over the bridge and leave his past behind him.

I suppose this is applicable for all seriously sinful lifestyles?

Right! Conversion to Christ is not merely intellectual, but involves the heart.

I suppose someone who made their living selling pornography would have to give up their profession.

That's correct.

How about fortunetellers?

Well, I'm sure you are not talking about cracking fortune cookies and reading the tiny slips of paper hidden inside. But if a person made their living as a fortuneteller, there would be a call for reform. Fortunetelling, spiritism, and other such things are clearly against the first commandment. People indulging in these occult practices attempt to pit themselves against God. They usurp divine powers, or at least pretend that they have powers beyond that of other human beings. A dollar-to-a-dime bet says this is a highly uncommon conversion in the United States.

Name some other incompatibilities.

Those who defraud for a living! Shysters! Flimflam artists! Prostitutes and pimps! Unmarried couples cohabiting! Bigamists! Hit men! Murderers! Abortionists and providers! Slave traders! Those who seriously exploit the poor! Whatever is blatantly un-Christlike has to go from a person's life before they can sincerely say, "I love you, Lord, and I will follow you."

Those who become Christians are not saints. You are not saying that they have to be perfect before being admitted to Christ's Church.

At the beginning of Mass, as Christians prepare to unite with Christ, they declare aloud their sinfulness. The penitential service is part of the eucharistic liturgy. There is an honest acknowledgment that they are sinners. Christ calls everyone to perfection. "Be perfect as your heavenly Father is perfect," he says. He instituted the sacrament of reconciliation, confession, to extend his mercy to those who have sinned since their baptism. Forgiveness is from the compassionate Christ. When people become Catholic, they know well that they are not perfect. They are, however, able to walk in harmony with God. They are able to remain in the state of grace. Converts to the faith cooperate with the grace of God in the months approaching their baptism. They begin to follow the Master.

This must be especially challenging to addicts and those who have cultivated vices.

God loves them. He gives graces according to one's state in life. Will power grows. Jesus is on their side. David slew Goliath because God was on his side. It can be done. Never underestimate the grace of God.

Something Extra

What is this ceremony called the Mass? What happens there?

The Mass—in which Jesus offers his own body and blood so that we might be redeemed from sin and in which Catholics take part as a sacred meal in which the Eucharist is consumed—is celebrated every day, but especially on a Sunday—the day of Jesus' Resurrection. The Mass has several parts: (1) the entrance rite in which people greet one another and prepare their minds for the celebration ahead; (2) the Liturgy of the Word, with readings, a homily, and intercessions; and (3) the Liturgy of the Eucharist, which consists of the presentation of bread and wine, and the consecration when the bread and wine are transubstantiated into Christ, his Body and Blood, which are received by the faithful in holy Communion.

The name *Mass* comes from the Latin word "*missio,*" meaning "the sending." This refers to the words of dismissal at the end of Mass: "*Ite missa est*"—"Go! It is sent forth," which in today's Mass is translated as "The Mass is ended, go in peace to love and serve the Lord."

CHAPTER TWENTY-TWO

Evangelization and Ecumenism

Is there a fear among evangelizers that in reaching out in Christ's name they might hinder the cause of ecumenism?

Ecumenism has to do with the goal of Christian unity. Why do you think that evangelization efforts would damage this cause?

Might not some pastors feel that their parishioners are being lured away into other religious denominations?

Some individual pastors may feel this way. But the essential mission of all Christian denominations is evangelization. Each denomination would not be true to its beliefs if it did not pursue the goal of eternal salvation for everyone.

It must be difficult for someone who begins to have interest in Jesus to have so many different Christian denominations competing for their attention. How confusing!

If someone came to Earth from another planet and became interested in Christ, it probably would be very challenging. They would walk down a street and see Catholic churches, Protestant churches, and Orthodox churches. No doubt all religions have devout and sincere members. However all Christian denominations do not believe in the same doctrines and do not relate to God in the same manner.

Division is not new among denominations. The centuries bear witness to the splintering of Christianity. Wouldn't this have an effect on evangelization?

The Church says this: "Divisions among Christians seriously impede the work of Christ.... This is one of the great obstacles to evangelization today. We desire collaboration with other Christian communities with whom we are not yet united in perfect unity. We take as a basis for this collaboration the foundation of Baptism and the patrimony of faith which is common to us. The duty of giving witness to the Gospel requires this" (*A Summary: On Evangelization in the Modern World*, §77).

That is a strong statement and a sad statement.

Christian unity is on the mind and in the heart of our Holy Father, the pope. Interdenominational commissions are organized for dialogue and discussion. The climate has improved in modern times. Prayer is needed to move the hearts of everyone involved. The Holy Spirit is needed to enlighten everyone.

How many religions are there in the world?

Hundreds! However, there are eight major religions: Hinduism, Buddhism, Taoism, Confucianism, Shintoism, Judaism, Christianity, and Islam. Generally speaking, the first five are located in the Orient. Judaism, Christianity, and Islam are more prevalent in the West.

Often in the United States there is reference made to Catholics, Jews, and Protestants. Are these three the predominant religions in this country?

Yes, generally speaking. However, due to immigration from the Orient and other countries, there are many followers of Islam, as well as members of the religions of the Orient.

How numerous are Catholics in the United States?

The *2000 Catholic Almanac* reports 62,018,436 Catholics in this country in 1999. This is the largest individual Christian Church. The Southern Baptists number about 15.7 million. Collectively, the many Protestant denominations exceed 100 million members. There are more than 250 Protestant Church bodies in the U.S.

When the different Christian denominations attempt to evangelize, do they invite men and women to follow Christ according to their own tradition?

Presumably, yes! They seek to interest men and women in following Christ according to the tradition and doctrines of their respective churches.

Are they successful?

In varying degrees. The evangelical Protestants, sometimes called fundamentalists, appear to be more successful, particularly in Latin American countries.

How successful are Catholics in evangelization?

The *2000 Catholic Almanac* statistics tell us that in 1999 there were: 1,044,837 infant baptisms; 73,426 adult baptisms, and 88,161 adults received into full communion in the Catholic Church in the United States.

Are there many people who are not listed in any church denomination?

There are millions who are not active members in any Christian community. They may be called unlisted, or even, un-

churched. Their values are not being reinforced by their regular attendance and association with any faith denomination. This does not mean that they are people without faith. Surveys show that the majority of people do pray, at least from time to time. Many would call themselves nominal Christians, that is, Christians in name. Perhaps they were baptized when they were young, but not reared in the faith. If asked, they are likely to identify themselves as Methodists, or Baptists, or Catholics, or another denomination, although their affiliation is principally in name.

When it comes to evangelization, what does the Catholic Church say about the great number who are not actively affiliated?

It says this: "The number of baptized who have not formally renounced their Baptism but who are indifferent to it and not living in accordance with it is very large. The resistance of this group to evangelization takes the form of inertia and the slightly hostile attitude of the person who feels that he or she is one of the family, but who claims to know and to have tried it all and no longer believes" (*A Summary: On Evangelization in the Modern World*, §56).

Most of the world is not Christian. The majority of those living on earth are members of other faiths. What is the Catholic Church's approach to the millions living in other countries?

Again Pope Paul VI says: "The Church respects and esteems non-Christian religions, because they are the living expression of the soul of vast groups of people. They possess an impressive religious patrimony. We wish to point out, however, that neither respect and esteem for these religions nor the complexity of the questions raised is an invitation to the Church to withhold from these non-Christians the proclamation of Jesus Christ" (*A Summary: On Evangelization in the Modern World*, §53). The evangelizer has to be sensitive and caring, but still imbued with the mission of spreading the Good News.

In simple terms, the evangelizer must be Christlike. What would Jesus do? How would he relate? Pope Paul VI says this:

"The Church also has a lively solicitude for Christians who are not in full communion with the Church. While preparing with them the unity willed by Christ, the Church would be gravely lacking if it did not give witness of the fullness of revelation whose deposit the Church guards" (*A Summary: On Evangelization in the Modern World*, §54).

Jesus prayed for unity at the Last Supper, on the night before he died. Ecumenism is a top priority. "Nevertheless," says Vatican II, "our separated brethren, whether considered as individuals or as communities and Churches, are not blessed with that unity which Jesus Christ wished to bestow on all those to whom he has given new birth into one body, and whom he has quickened to newness of life— that unity which the Holy Scriptures and the ancient Tradition of the Church proclaim. For it is through Christ's Catholic Church alone, which is the universal help towards salvation, that the fullness of the means of salvation can be obtained" (*Unitatis Redintegratio*, "Decree on Ecumenism," §3).

Something Extra

What are some ways to proclaim Christ at work?

- On the job, actively listen to others without judgment.

- Practice charity through giving others the benefit of the doubt.

- Quietly answer anti-Catholic sentiments by taking the speaker aside and offering to correct any misinterpretations.

- Be generous to work colleagues.

- Actively champion pro-life points of view.

- Pray privately for your fellow workers and their families.

- Without embarrassment, mention your faith life in casual conversations—fasting on the Fridays of Lent, attendance at Mass on holy days of obligation, reception of ashes on Ash Wednesday.

- Give short shrift to gossip. Respect the reputation of others.

- Uphold the truth in all circumstances.

- Demonstrate personal respect for all people.

CHAPTER TWENTY-THREE

Mary and the Saints

So is it possible that all those in the hundreds of religions are going to be saved for eternity? Some say, quite cavalierly, that we are all going to the same place anyway.

How can anyone know? Eternity depends on our free cooperation with the grace of God. God does look on the sincerity of one's heart. It is possible for everyone to gain eternal salvation. There is no revelation on this matter, however.

You do hold that regardless of a person's religious affiliation, if he or she is going to be with God in paradise, it will be through the merits and mediation of Jesus Christ. You have cited Christ's words. "I am the way, and the truth, and the life. No one comes to the Father except through me" (Jn 14:15).

Yes! Jesus is the one Mediator. All of us experience the mercy and beneficence of God through Jesus Christ. This rings true for everyone on the face of the earth. "For there is one God, / there is also one mediator between God and humankind, / Christ Jesus, himself human, / who gave himself a ransom for all" (1 Tim 2:5-6).

Yet Catholics call Mary the Mediatrix of Graces.

Vatican II explains her role in this way: "The maternal duty of Mary toward men in no way obscures or diminishes this unique mediation of Christ, but rather shows its power." Mary is invoked under the titles of Advocate, Auxiliatrix, Adjurix, and Mediatrix. "This, however, is so understood that it neither takes away anything from nor adds anything to the dignity and efficacy of Christ the one Mediator"(*Lumen Gentium*, "Dogmatic Constitution on the Church," §62).

This reflects a strong relationship between Mary, Jesus' mother, and his work of redemption.

A very strong and unique relationship! This began with Christ's words on the cross. He entrusted his mother to John. He entrusted John to his mother. "Mother, behold your son. Son, behold your mother." Just as Mary served God in being the mother of his divine Son, so she has continued in her loving relationship with John.

So this relationship to Mary has been integral to the Catholic Church from the beginning?

Yes. Vatican II explains it this way: "By reason of the gift and role of her divine motherhood, by which she is united with her Son, the Redeemer, and with her unique graces and functions, the Blessed Virgin is also intimately united to the Church....The Church, therefore, in her apostolic work too, rightly looks to her who gave birth to Christ, who was thus conceived of the Holy Spirit and born of a virgin, in order that through the Church he could be born and increase in the hearts of the faithful" (*Lumen Gentium*,"Dogmatic Constitution on the Church," §63, 65).

So is Mary herself an evangelizer?

An evangelizer is one who brings Christ to people. Mary, in the fullest sense of the word, has brought Christ to all of us.

Usually we think of evangelizers as those who preach to us.

This is true. Preaching is a primary way to communicate Christ. Many of those that we honor as saints distinguished themselves by preaching. Saint Paul was indefatigable. Missionaries to foreign countries carry the "good news" to those who never heard of Christ. For example, Saint Peter Chanel, born in France in 1803, journeyed to Oceania and to the islands of Futuna where the name of Christ had never been preached. A companion, a lay brother, spoke of his dedication: "Because of his labors he was often burned by the heat of the sun, and famished with hunger, and he would return home wet with perspiration and completely exhausted. Yet he always remained in good spirits, courageous and energetic." Saint Peter, by his preaching, destroyed a cult of evil spirits and eventually was martyred by local chieftains. Still, he so firmly established the Church in Futuna and the other islands that Christianity flourishes there.

Parishioners, the men and women in the pews, ordinarily think evangelization belongs to priests and missionaries.

It would be helpful if they began to consider that it is their apostolate, too. If we ask ourselves what can we do to please Jesus, surely he would say that communicating the good news of salvation, declaring the kingdom of God, sharing our faith, are important aspects of our relationship with him. One of the difficulties might be that parishioners live among other Christians. They do not see the burning need to communicate the faith to those who already have the faith. Nevertheless, there are many people whose lives are empty. They do not know God. They do not know Jesus. They do not have a genu-

ine relationship with the Father through Jesus. It is not good for parishioners to think that evangelization is not their job. They can be very instrumental channels of God's grace.

Why do many parishioners fail to see that they are called to evangelize?

Perhaps they have not been challenged. No one has encouraged them to seek out those without faith. They may be very sincere and dedicated in practicing their faith, but evangelizing has not been cultivated in their lives. Many Catholics learn their prayers, attend religious education classes as they are growing up, and worship regularly on Sundays. Students in Catholic schools are more likely to have heard about missionaries and their activities than those in public schools. Evangelization is for those in faraway places with strange-sounding names.

Then is it a matter of perspective that many Catholics are not trained to evangelize—that they are not strongly motivated in their hearts to share faith in Christ?

In many Catholic parishes there are no particular programs of recruiting new converts. Other denominations may focus on seeking out the unchurched. The Mormons, that is, members of the Church of Latter Day Saints, do have a training program for their young adults. These young people devote themselves to person-to-person contact for a two-year period of time.

Are you in favor of a similar effort among Catholic parishioners?

There is renewed interest in evangelization among American bishops. They have emphasized the need to evangelize. These prelates, through their united efforts as the National Council of Catholic Bishops, have published a document called *Go and Make Disciples.* There are many good efforts being made in dioceses in the country. There are conferences and workshops. Some individual parishes and dioceses have sponsored door-to-door visitation and/or census-taking. There has not been a specific program akin to the missionary program of the Mormons. Some parish priests manage to visit the homes of parishioners. They make some contacts through neighborhood visitation. There is a congregation of nuns called Parish Visitors of Mary Immaculate. These religious women have been reaching out in an unassuming, quiet, but effective way for years. They may be reached at P.O. Box 658, Monroe, NY 10950.

Do you see a need to quicken the appreciation of parishioners for evangelization?

The *Sacramentary*, the large book used on the altar, has this prayer in a votive Mass, for the spread of the Gospel. "Father, you will your Church to be the sacrament of salvation for all peoples. Make us feel more urgently the call to work for the salvation of all men, until you have made us all one people. Inspire the hearts of all your people to continue the saving work of Christ everywhere until the end of the world." So we do wish to feel the urgency to tell the world about the world's greatest historical event ...the coming of God's Son, Jesus.

Something Extra

What are some questions to ask in preparing a personal story of faith?

In his excellent book, *The Evangelizing Catholic*, Frank P. DeSiano, C.S.P., gives some starting questions for putting our own story of faith into words:

When did I realize that I actually had faith and not just a superficial belief?

What or who was responsible for this occurrence?

When did I first know that God was real to me?

What were some of the most significant religious experiences of my life?

How have my religious convictions changed throughout my life?

Has someone—a spiritual director, a friend—or something—a book, a personal crisis—played an important role in this change?

What sayings or scriptural stories have come to affect me most deeply?

What are my hopes in living out my faith?

How has God helped me in my life? Has he comforted me in my fears? Answered my longings?

How do I live out in my life my belief in God. Do my actions and values support this belief?

CHAPTER TWENTY-FOUR

How Simple Is Evangelization?

So is evangelization really that simple?

It is simple from the standpoint that every Christian can do his part. The evangelized Christian, a person who truly appreciates and loves Jesus, wishes to share this treasure, this faith with others. He tells the non-Christians and nonpracticing Christians that Jesus is the light of his life. He finds a way to proclaim Christ. He lives "the way" of Christ and communicates his appreciation of God's tremendous love in sending his Son.

Not all Christians are doing this. My guess is that a great percentage have never done this. Am I right?

Yes, but all the more reason to do everything possible to evangelize. Says Pope Paul VI: "Evangelizers, be worthy of your vocation. Exercise it without doubt or fear. Do not neglect the conditions that will make your vocation active and fruitful" (*A Summary: On Evangelization in the Modern World,* §74).

I suppose evangelizers must feel they are working hand in hand with God and they cannot lose?

God wishes Christians to communicate, to share their faith. Evangelizers do not work alone. "The Holy Spirit is the principal agent of evangelization. It is he who inspires each individual to proclaim the Gospel, and it is he who causes the word of salvation to be understood and accepted" (*A Summary: On Evangelization in the Modern World,* §75).

Can evangelization really be simplified?

Since God wishes the participation of every Christian, evangelization can be explained. Its language can be made understandable. The process is clear. Human beings cooperate with God. Writings articulate the challenges that underlie evangelization. We do well not to underestimate the challenges, however. "Evangelization, therefore, is a complex process made up of varied elements: the renewal of humanity, witness, explicit proclamation, inner adherence, entry into the community, acceptance of signs and apostolic initiative" (*A Summary: On Evangelization in the Modern World*, §24).

Tell me a little bit about the phrase, "entry into the community."

It is Jesus who organized his followers. He established the Catholic Church. Jesus identifies with his Church. "Remember, I am with you always, to the end of the age" (Mt 28:20). Jesus said, "For where two or three are gathered in my name, I am there among them" (Mt 18:20). Christ's Church is a family of faith, a community of believers. Through baptism we become children of God.

There are those who are against "organized religion."

That's simply a "cop-out." It is Christ's will that we belong to his family of faith. There are thousands of Catholic parishes throughout the world. Their common bond is Jesus Christ himself. Each and every parish in every country is linked with Jesus Christ. There is a divine presence. There is Christ's physical presence, his sacramental presence, in the Blessed Sacrament. Together with Jesus, the parishes and parishioners are a faith community.

So the evangelizers worldwide are saying welcome to our world?

Saint Cyril of Jerusalem (A.D. 315–386) put it this way: "The Catholic Church is the distinctive name of this holy Church which is the mother of us all. She is the bride of our Lord, Jesus Christ, the only begotten Son of God (for Scripture says: Christ loved the Church and gave himself up for her). She is the type and bears the image of the Jerusalem above all that is free and is the mother of us all, that Jerusalem which was once barren but now has many children."

Saint Cyril was a great teacher. Even in the fourth century he clarified thoughts about the Church. "The Church is called Catholic or universal because it has spread throughout the entire world, from one end of the earth to the other. Again, it is called Catholic because it teaches fully and unfailingly the doctrine which ought to be brought to men's knowledge, whether concerned with visible or invisible things, with realities of heaven or the things of earth." Cyril articulated in a straightforward and simple manner that the Catholic Church is the faith community of Christ. He showed in his writings that there had to be harmony among members. Their faith united them.

What is the simplest approach an evangelizer can have?

God loves you. He sent his Son into our world so that we might have eternal life.

After that it is just a matter of filling in the details?

The evangelizer continues to assist in the person's journey of faith. God's grace is at work. There is an inner transformation, a conversion. They work hand in hand. The candidate for Christianity has to have it all come together in mind and heart.

So is this process the same for men and women in all countries throughout the world? Are there different customs and mentalities since human beings differ from one another ethnically and in languages?

The Holy Spirit enlightens souls. The Holy Spirit strengthens them in their challenges. Each individual can succeed with the grace of God.

So is there greater success in terms of numbers when a country is economically strong and the inhabitants enjoy the basic necessities of life?

There are times when people pay less attention to God. When they have an abundance of material goods, they do not always turn to God for their needs. They ease themselves into a false sense of security. Good times may or may not be ideal for conversion to God.

Do you favor trying times—conditions that are less advantageous for the spread of the faith?

No! There is no need to second-guess God. It is good to realize that God's grace is sufficient at all times. He blesses people with the graces that they need according to their challenges. For example a newspaper article about the Catholic Church in China notes that China's millions of Catholics have experienced years of intense hardship at the hands of a Communist government. Even though the Church's activities are completely illegal in China, and Catholics can be im-

prisoned, beaten, or even killed for practicing the faith, the Church has known unprecedented growth—a tripling of members in the same five decades in which the Church has known only opposition.

God's ways certainly are mysterious, aren't they?

The human mind is no match for God and his infinite wisdom. There is insight into God's thinking, however. Evangelizers do well to read the gospels prayerfully. Jesus explained things clearly. He declared that he came to bear witness to the truth. He said, "If you have seen me, you have seen the Father." Evangelizers and those who are evangelized can often see quite clearly.

Something Extra

From past experience Catholics are often inward looking instead of outward looking. Here are some suggestions for activities that may potentially present opportunities for personal evangelization.

- Be a door-to-door canvasser on your block for the Cancer Society, the Heart Fund, or the March of Dimes

- Coach a Little League or other community sports team

- Assist on a volunteer basis in a local political campaign—or better yet, be a candidate

- Train to serve on a distress hot line

- Join a special-interest club

- Take a popular night-school course that will have a wide spectrum of people in attendance

- Invite neighbors to a block party

- Join a community program that supports a particular cause—a crisis nursery, the Big Sisters, and so on

- Volunteer at the local hospital

CHAPTER TWENTY-FIVE

Why Does God Communicate The Way He Does?

Why does God entrust the essential mission of Christ and his Church to us?

Because it is the best way to evangelize. God does not make mistakes.

Humans are weak. Their minds are darkened because of original sin. There are hundreds of languages and dialects. Men and women do not always think clearly. Pride and prejudice affect their judgments. You would almost think that there would have to be a better way.

God is mindful of human nature. He created it. God understands the full scope of the consequences of original sin. God entered a relationship with his creatures. He made people after his image and likeness so that they could communicate with him and he could communicate with them. God's holy will was made known from the beginning of time.

How did God communicate from the very beginning?

The Letter to the Hebrews explains it in this way: "Long ago God spoke to our ancestors in many and various ways by the prophets, but in these last days he has spoken to us by a Son, whom he appointed heir of all things, through whom he also created the worlds. He is the reflection of God's glory and the exact imprint of God's very being, and he sustains all things by his powerful word. When he had made purification for sins, he sat down at the right hand of the Majesty on high, having become as much superior to angels as the name he has inherited is more excellent than theirs"(Heb 1:1-4).

Break that quotation down for me.

There are books of the Old Testament of the Bible that explain how God dealt with people in ancient times. God inspired prophets and holy men and women to lead. In time, God chose Abraham to be the Father of his chosen people, the Jews. Their history traces Abraham's children and descendants, their lineage, up to the birth of Jesus Christ. The books of the New Testament render an account of God's communication in Christ's time. God chose to send his Son Jesus who is a divine Person, both God and man. God comes in person. There is no greater communication than this.

So we know the mind of God more clearly and accurately through his Son. The Bible is a cherished account. Where would we be without the Bible?

It is important to understand that we have a living voice, God's voice. The Bible is not the sole rule or norm of faith. God has not ceased to guide his people. The Bible, Tradition, and the Church are one. This is brought out in the documents of Vatican Council II. People are not going about hearing voices. Nevertheless, God continues to guide his flock through Jesus, the Good Shepherd.

Articulate this a little more, please.

There have been general councils, ecumenical councils, of the Church through the centuries. The popes teach and write authentically. The bishops, in harmony with the Holy Father, preach and teach individually and collectively. The American bishops issue timely statements on the current challenges to the faith and to society. They speak out on the right to life, the importance of the family and the home, and, of course, on evangelization. They are like the prophets of old, echoing God's voice.

You are not minimizing the importance of the Bible are you?

Not at all. The Bible is God's holy word. It is a wonderful record of God's communication down through the centuries. There is a need, however, to interpret God's word with God's authority. That's why it is correct to say that God communicates through his word, through Tradition, and through the Church. This is the way God communicates and it is the best way.

Do you think that the message is presented with the greatest plausibility?

What else can we expect from God in order to communicate his love? He has sent his Son. Nothing is more convincing than Jesus' life and teachings. His miracles and Resurrection demonstrate his divinity. No one can love us more.

Yet there are people who have heard of Jesus and do not become followers.

God respects the freedom with which he has endowed human beings. God is love, as Saint John tells us. Love is never coerced. Jesus invites people to "Come follow me." All the conditions and human dispositions have to be right for men and women to respond. The Holy Spirit supports their decisions, acting concomitantly. We must not forget a conversion process

that takes place in the soul. With God's grace they take up their crosses and follow Christ. Everything necessary to win their hearts freely is done by our loving Lord.

So evangelization works in a mysterious manner?

God touches the human heart. God's ways are indeed mysterious. If Jesus came from God, and is God as well as man, his divine presence should be persuasive and convincing. This is divine intervention. This is God acting on earth.

Jesus told an interesting parable about a rich man who was dressed in purple and fine linen. The man ate and drank sumptuously every day. He lived the good life. At this rich man's gate there was a beggar named Lazarus who longed to eat the scraps from the rich man's table. Dogs came and licked the poor man's sores. Eventually both men died. Lazarus went to heaven, that is, to be with Abraham. The rich man went to hell, the nether world, where there was utter misery. He pleaded with Abraham to send Lazarus, "to dip the tip of his finger in water and cool my tongue, for I am in agony in these flames." Abraham explained that there was no going from heaven to hell and vice versa. The rich man appealed to have Lazarus return to earth to warn the rich man's five brothers so they would not suffer the same fate. Abraham said that his brothers had Moses and the prophets to guide them. The rich man pleaded to have Abraham to send Lazarus himself, "someone from the dead." Abraham replied, "If they do not listen to Moses and the prophets, neither will they be convinced even if someone rises from the dead" (Lk 16:19–31).

Nice story! It was almost as if Jesus knew that his own Resurrection would not prove convincing to some people.

God communicates well. Now he expects Christians to carry the message. He entrusts the "good news" to Jesus' followers. Evangelization is commissioned. Evangelizers work harmoniously with God.

This is not just a figure of speech or a theological nicety, is it?

The more this harmonious relationship is studied, the greater it is understood and appreciated. The ordained priest, for example, speaks in the person of Christ. In the confessional he says "I absolve you from your sins." At the altar, taking the bread and wine he declares, "This is my body" and "This is the cup of my blood." Christ speaks though the priest. Moreover, all the baptized are called "a priestly people." Christians are members of Christ's Body, the Church. And the Church is called the "Sacrament of Salvation." You can see the thread of thought weaving through the fabric. The Bible, holy Tradition, and the Church are truly an expression of God and God communicating.

In summary, a quotation from the decree on missionary activity of the Church issued by the Second Vatican Council says this: "The Lord Jesus, before giving his life freely for the world, made his arrangements for the apostolic ministry, and gave his promise that the Holy Spirit was to be sent. He did this in such a way that both the Spirit and ministry might be partners in carrying into effect the work of salvation in every age and place.

"The Holy Spirit gives to the

whole Church at all times unity in communion and ministry. He endows it with a diversity of gifts, hierarchical and charismatic; he gives life to its institutions, becoming as it were their soul, and instills into the hearts of the faithful the very missionary spirit that was the driving force in Christ himself. At times he is seen preparing the way for apostolic activity, just as in different ways he always accompanies it and directs it.

"The Lord Jesus, from the very beginning, called to himself those whom he wanted; he arranged for twelve to be with him, and to be sent by him to preach. Thus the apostles were the first beginnings of the new Israel, and at the same time the origin of the sacred hierarchy.

"Afterward, when he had once and for all, by his death and resurrection, brought to completion in his own person the mysteries of salvation and the renewal of all things, the Lord, having received all power in heaven and on earth, before he was taken up to heaven, founded his Church as the sacrament of salvation, and sent the apostles into the whole world, just as he had been sent by the Father. He commanded them: Go then and teach all nations, baptizing them in the name of the Father and of the Son and of the Holy Spirit, teaching them to observe all things that I have commanded you.

"From then on there is a duty laid on the Church of spreading the faith and salvation that come from Christ. This duty is in virtue of the express command inherited from the apostles by the college of bishops, assisted by the priests, in communion with Peter's successor, the chief of the Church; it is in virtue also of the life that Christ causes to flow into his members.

"The mission of the Church is therefore fulfilled by that activity by which the Church, in obedience to Christ's command and under the impulse of grace and love of the Holy Spirit, becomes fully and actively present to all men and to all peoples, to lead them by the example of its life, by its preaching, by the sacraments and other means of grace, to the faith, freedom and peace of Christ, so that therein lies open before them a free and firm path to a full sharing in the mystery of Christ."

Something Extra

Prayer

Thank you, Jesus, for allowing us to assist you in saving souls. You permit us to work side by side with you in the world's most important task, the redemption of every person. This is divine love. This is divine mercy. This is divine compassion.

The heavenly Father sends you to be our "great news." You are the cause of our joy. The Holy Spirit guides us in freedom, encourages us to love every man, woman, and child because you love them. You came that all nations and peoples might form a single family, a community of faith. Inspire us to be truly Christian, to walk faithfully in your footsteps. Your goal and our goal are one.

Strengthen us in our resolve to complete this essential mission. This happens when we are totally dedicated as you are totally dedicated. Love reaches its fulfillment in giving, in sacrifice.

May your words on the cross, Jesus, resound in our ears and echo across the world. "It is finished" (Jn 19:30). Evangelization is accomplished by your grace. Amen.

Resources

Organizations:

United States Catholic Conference
3211 Fourth Street, NE
Washington, DC 20017-1194
(800) 235-8722 for catalog.

Paulist National Catholic Evangelization Association
3031 Fourth Street NE
Washington, DC 20017
1-800237-5515 for catalog.

Contact your local Catholic Dioceses. Some have developed programs of evangelization.

Catholics Come Home Program
Roman Catholic Diocese of Phoenix
400 East Monroe Street
Phoenix, AZ 85004-2376

National Council for Catholic Evangelization
P.O. Box 1260
South Holland, IL 60473-1260
1-800-786-NCCE

Publications:

Blum, Susan. *Share Your Faith: A Behavioral Approach for Evangelization Training.* Boca Raton: Jeremiah Press, 1990.

Brennan, Patrick J. *The Evangelizing Parish: Theologies and Strategies for Renewal* (Allen, Tex.: Tabor Publishing Co., 1987).

DeSiano, C.S.P., Frank. *The Evangelizing Catholic: A Practical Handbook for Reaching Out.* Mahway, N.J.: Paulist Press, 1998.

DeSiano, C.S.P., Frank. *Presenting the Catholic Faith: A Modern Catechism for Inquirers.* Mahwah, N.J.: Paulist Press, 1987.

DeSiano, C.S.P., Frank. *Sowing New Seed: Directions for Evangelization Today.* Mahwah, N.J.: Paulist Press, 1994.

DeSiano, C.S.P., Frank and Kenneth Boyack, C.S.P. *Creating the Evangelizing Parish.* Mahwah, N.J.: Paulist Press, 1993.

Illig, Alvin A. *A Summary: On Evangelization in the Modern World.* Washington, D.C.: Paulist National Evangelization Association, n.d.

Kemp, Carrie and Donald Pologruto. *Catholics Coming Home: A Handbook for Churches Reaching Out to Inactive Catholics,* San Francisco: HarperSF, 1990.

Plus, S.J., Raoul. *Winning Souls for Christ: How You Can Become an Effective Apostle.* Manchester, N.H.: Sophia Institute Press, 1999.

APPENDIX

Sample Copy for Leaflets

Would You Like to Become a Catholic?

Would you like to become a follower of Jesus Christ? A member of his Church? You are most welcome!

The word *catholic* derives from the Greek word *katholikos,* which means "universal." Jesus commissioned his apostles: "Go therefore and make disciples of all nations, baptizing them in the name of the Father and of the Son and of the Holy Spirit, and teaching them to obey everything that I have commanded you" (Mt 28:19-20). They were to bring the "Good News" of God's love to every person. In A.D. 110 Saint Ignatius, Bishop of Antioch, declared: "Where Jesus Christ is, there is the Catholic Church." Ignatius succeeded Saint Peter who established the Church in Antioch before going on to Rome.

Jesus Christ is true God and true man, a divine Person, the second Person of the Trinity. He is our Redeemer and our Savior. He declared, "I am the way, and the truth, and the life. No one comes to the Father except through me" (Jn 14:6). Jesus exemplifies and defines our relationship with God.

If you are not a Catholic, we are happy to assist you in your journey of faith. The answers to life come from Jesus Christ. Origin and destiny? Where did we come from? Where are we going? How do we get there? Saint Augustine, many centuries ago, exclaimed, "Our souls are restless, O Lord, and they will not rest until they rest in thee."

155

If you are already a practicing Catholic, pray for God's graces and blessings for those not yet embraced by Christ in his family of faith. Offer assistance to those alienated or separated from the Church.

Share This Card!

"For God so loved the world that he gave his only Son, so that everyone who believes in him may not perish but may have eternal life" (Jn 3:16).

(Give contact person of organization here.)

Sample Copy for Leaflets

I Am a Catholic Because...

I am a Catholic because I have come to know Jesus Christ, and I believe in him. He is the Messiah, the one sent by the heavenly Father, to redeem us. Jesus proved, beyond a shadow of a doubt that, he, too, is God with the Father and the Holy Spirit. There is one God in whom there are three divine Persons.

I believe in Jesus because of his miracles, and because of his teaching, which are unsurpassable and sublime. His way of life matches, endorses, his teachings.

I believe in Jesus because he is love itself. His sufferings and death are clear signs of his love, the ultimate sacrifice, reconciling me in a loving relationship with the heavenly Father. He forgives my sins. I cherish the crucifix. I believe in Jesus because he declared, "I am the way, and the truth, and the life. No one comes to the Father except through me" (Jn 14:6).

I believe in Jesus because he promises everlasting life. "I am the resurrection and the life. Those who believe in me, even though they die, will live, and everyone who lives and believes in me will never die" (Jn 11:25). This gives me comfort and contentment in my present life's journey, my pilgrimage of faith.

I am Catholic because I want to be one with Christ, especially, and particularly, by receiving Jesus in holy Communion. "I am the bread of life...for my flesh is true food and my blood is true drink....If you do not eat the flesh of the Son of Man and drink his blood, you have no life in you" (Jn 6).

There are many more compelling reasons for believing in Jesus Christ and belonging to his Church. Every baptized Catholic is encouraged to share his or her faith. Personalize your story. Make it sincerely your own. Sharing the treasure of your faith is an act of love. "It was in Antioch that the disciples were first called 'Christians'" (Acts 11:26). Saint Ignatius, Bishop of Antioch, declared in A.D. 110: "Where Jesus Christ is, there is the Catholic Church." I believe in Jesus' Church, his family of faith. He continues to guide and direct it. "I am with you always, to the end of the age" (Mt 28:20).

May we assist you in your journey of faith? We pray that this card is a help in sharing the "Good News," the gospel of Jesus Christ. Your local parish priests have a welcome mat at the door and are delighted to serve you. For more information, contact (person or organization).